AFTER THE WEDDING

AFTER THE WEDDING

Philip Yancey

WORD BOOKS, Publisher   Waco, Texas

First Printing—December 1976
Second Printing—August 1977

ISBN 0-87680-456-3
Library of Congress catalog card number: 76-19537
Printed in the United States of America

Scripture quotations marked *The Living Bible*
are taken from *The Living Bible, Paraphrased*
(Wheaton: Tyndale House Publishers, 1971) and
are used by permission.

Let us stop just saying we love people; let us really love them, and show it by our actions.

1 John 3:18, *The Living Bible*

CONTENTS

FOREWORD

If you were curious about the divorce rate of left-handed Puerto Rican nudists who married midget Caucasians wearing dental braces, I imagine you could find a chart which would give you those statistics. Marriage is surely the most analyzed, talked-about, dissected institution in this country.

There's only one problem. Few people read the information on marriage. Plenty of facts and principles and guidelines are available to help a struggling couple, but generally they're both written and read by sociologists, psychologists, pastors, and marriage counselors. Those of us who are just married, but have no professional skills, can barely interpret the jargon the great truths hide behind.

Christian literature on marriage presents a unique dilemma. To explain, let me tell you how I decided to write this book. As I write this, my own marriage is approaching its fifth anniversary, a disadvantage to one who's writing about marriage, but an advantage to one who's writing about only the first five years of marriage. The headaches, clashes, struggles, triumphs, and intimacies are yesterday-fresh to me.

As Janet and I were sliding and soaring through the first five years, we set out to find other young couples who might be mirroring our experiences. Perhaps together we could profit by sharing.

9

Our group did share, but we had difficulty finding books to help us. The Christian books eloquently described abstract principles such as submission and mutuality and intimacy, with appropriate Bible references and footnotes referring to sociology surveys. But the meaningful times of our group occurred, not when we studied the books, but when someone was courageous enough to say, "Hold it. Let's stop talking philosophy and abstracts. My wife and I had a terrible week. We've been at each other's throats, and we need help. We can't get perspective on this problem." Immediately that struck a chord of response inside us. Chances were, another couple had been through or were currently going through the very same problem.

I had an idea. Was there a way to capture verbally the struggle and triumph of the incredible process of male and female coming together? And if I could do that, wouldn't the principles and abstractions fit directly into the experiences I described? And so, as I reflected, the format of this book evolved.

The nine couples you will read about are real people. Most had been married about five years when I interviewed them. I asked them to share not what they thought their marriages should be like, but what it was actually like.

Most of the couples are my close friends. They agreed with this project and willingly lowered their protective barriers in hopes of helping you in your own marriage pilgrimage. Believing a geographical sampling would be necessary for authenticity, I traveled all over the country to interview them. (I used pseudonyms in the chapters, at the request of some of the couples, and I have changed some facts, such as place names, where requested.)

These nine marriages are not ideal marriages, but most are marriages which work. Despite conflicts, most of the couples really love each other and are pulling together to construct a satisfying future. All are Christians. I thank them for baring themselves to me and to you.

As I worked on the book, I was struck with the very phenomenon of marriage. That two people could come together so as to become a separate third person, despite all the sandpaper-grating and sparks and bulges and explosions that occur when any two people rub closely—that is a phenomenon.

Why the First Five Years?

To someone married twenty years or more, the first five years of marriage may seem like a mere warmup exercise, an interesting period of coming together with little organic relevance to the rich, mature years of later marriage. But to a couple exploring the first five years, nothing is more important than those years. If they can't survive the initial trials together, there will be no rich, mature future.

When do you think the divorce rate hits the highest peak? Consider this graph of divorce occurrence, as reported by Dr. Bernard Harnik: [1]

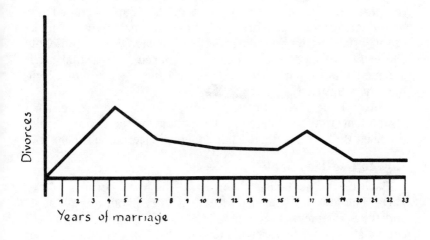

FREQUENCY OF DIVORCE
AS RELATED TO DURATION OF MARRIAGE.

Moreover, Dr. Harnik reports that since he compiled this graph the divorce rate has slipped backwards so that the peak is now between the third and fourth year of marriage.

What happens? What goes wrong?

I'm convinced that the first five years contain too many surprises for couples. Personalities differ and soon one partner begins storing up resentments. Perhaps he feels betrayed because his partner seems to act differently now than before he married. Perhaps he feels trapped because his partner wraps tight emotional tentacles around him.

One of the foremost marriage counselors in the world, David Mace, reports, "Auto mechanics tell us that the way a car is treated in the first thousand miles will have a deep and lasting influence on the way it behaves later. Something like that is true also of the marriage relationship. We now know that the shape of a marriage develops quite early. In the first six or twelve months a couple develops habits of behaving toward one another that become settled and are not easily changed later. These habits decide a number of important questions: who plays the dominant and who the submissive role, who takes major responsibility for the different areas of the couple's shared life, how quarrels are handled, who initiates the first move to make up, who makes the final decision in what areas, how household chores are allocated, how money is managed, how sexual needs are met, relationships with in-laws or former friends or neighbors, how leisure time is spent." [2]

With all these adjustments, it's easy to see why patterns of resentment develop! These are the same areas these nine couples thrashed through together. I hope their pioneering will help you.

How to Use This Book

Each of the next nine chapters of this book consists of two parts. The first, the longer part, tells a story about a real couple and the adjustments they must make to live together. Because a couple always has two viewpoints, not one, I have told the stories in dialogue form.

Each story is followed by various principles which relate to problems discussed by the couple. I am not a marriage expert, I am a journalist, so I have scoured many books to extract these principles. I'm aware that conclusions to chapters labeled "For Further Thought" or "Actions to Take" are usually skipped by an impatient reader, so I have tried to keep these comments succinct and interesting. Each principle meshes with an incident in the story.

Many marriage books use illustrations from real couples, but they use them as parenthetical material, seeded in to illustrate a principle. In contrast, I will begin with the couple and their story, then add on a few principles to add perspective. Hopefully, the result will be more readable.

Because this book is of a unique format, I recommend the following approach in using it:

1. Read one chapter at a sitting. Each chapter is a single unit, with the story of a marriage and principles relating to it. Reading too many at once would tend to clutter and fog the principles of adjustment.

2. Use the questions at the conclusion of the chapters; discuss them with your spouse.

3. Join or start a marriage growth group. David Mace is convinced that the real agents of change in marriage are not the books and records and cassettes and filmstrips, but other people with whom we become involved. I hope the technique of presenting live models to consider in each chapter will inch toward that goal. But the book could become much more meaningful if you use it as a springboard to share your experiences with other growing couples.

4. Don't stop here. If you want to go deeper, please dig out recommended sources from the bibliography. Paul Tournier and Charlie Shedd are probably the most readable Christian writers on marriage. (Whatever you do, don't skip the Appendix, which contains interviews with those two delightful men and their wives.)

5. If you need professional help, seek it out from your pastor or a qualified counselor. One of the big surprises to me in compiling this book was finding out that over half of the couples had sought some kind of professional counseling, either as individuals or as couples. You'll read about some of the results. At last, perhaps, it is not considered an opprobrium to admit, "I need help."

*I had walked into marriage expecting a
finished house. Instead, I found that much
building needed to be done; we were only
given the shell. But I had no tools. I didn't
know where to begin and I wasn't at all
sure I wanted to.*

CHAPTER ONE

No Tools

CURT AND PAULA ABBOTT

Curt and Paula Abbott shared a classic romance. They met
when the front door fell off Paula's apartment while Curt was
working as a maintenance man. He responded to her frantic plea
for help, and there soon began an exciting, pulsing bond between
them which eventually led to marriage. Curt had scarcely considered the option of marriage: as with much of life, he avoided
thinking about it until the decision bore down on him. For
Paula, though, getting married was the ultimate, every girl's
dream.

One year after the wedding, however, the Abbotts' marriage
was in shambles. Paula had become, in her words, "a whimper-
ing, complaining housewife who insisted on making all the decisions." Curt responded by looking for excuses to avoid coming
home. He rarely talked to Paula, he felt uncomfortable around
her friends.

Paula said, "If we had sat down and thought about our goals
and expectations of life, I know we'd never have gotten married.
We seemed to slide into it, like sliding down a gentle toboggan
run until finally—slap!—we hit an icy lake at the end of the
run and realized we'd made a mistake. I'm convinced we both
married the wrong people. We could hardly be worse for each
other."

The Abbotts' experience is typical of young couples who

"fall in love" and then, with little preparation, drift into a relationship. "I spent more time picking out Paula's wedding ring than thinking about our compatibility," Curt says.

Together, the Abbotts endured much emotional pain and bitterness. But they survived intact and now have a healthy, God-based relationship. For that to happen, both Curt and Paula had to undergo drastic changes. Their story serves as a model for couples who suddenly wake up and find they married the wrong person. There can be an alternative to divorce: listen to the Abbotts.

PAULA: I suppose I've always been somewhat of a boy-chaser. Preachers' daughters tend to attract the attention of guys in church, and I usually led them on. Their advances flattered me.

After I had left home and gotten a job on my own near Chicago, I began to feel frantic. I suppose every single girl in her twenties succumbs to the pressure of worrying *Will I be passed by? What if no one ever asks me to marry him? Is something wrong with me?*

From that first meeting over my broken front door, Curt appealed to me. He was short and slim, with shiny black hair and a cute goatee, which he would stroke as he talked. He stood stiffly, always looking as if he were about to clear his throat. I learned he majored in engineering at the University of Wisconsin and that heightened my interest. (My preacher's kid rebellious streak perked up at the chance to know someone so "secular.")

I had watched Curt move into our apartment complex, and had been dying for a chance to meet him. Curt was shy and reserved and, irritatingly, he didn't seem to notice my existence at first.

CURT: I had moved to Wheaton for a summer to work at the National Accelerator Laboratory, and I anticipated a quiet, reflective summer. It was the late '60s, when student violence and protest had peaked. Kids would stay up late at night in the dorms discussing revolution. A bomb at our University Math Center had killed one grad student. I didn't fall into the violent crowd, but I had taken up smoking pot, drinking, and visiting topless nightclubs.

Straying from my moral upbringing had made me feel uncomfortable and slightly guilty. Now, away from my friends and the pressures of university life, I had hoped to become more serious and searching. I wasn't quite ready for Wheaton, though. I walked two blocks to explore the Wheaton College campus, and was greeted by a giant rock with these words chiseled in it: "For Christ and His Kingdom." I laughed out loud. It seemed like something out of the nineteenth century.

PAULA: Even though Curt's secularness excited me, I knew it was my duty as a Christian to try to convert him. (I had been programmed to see every person I met as a potential convert.)

Several weeks later, over a cup of coffee, I told him why I was a Christian and what God meant to me. I was impressed that he listened so intently. He asked intelligent questions, including some I'd never considered. But he didn't reject what I said.

We started going to church together and we began dating sporadically, playing tennis or going into Chicago. Curt never showed his emotions much, but he was always polite and seemed interested in me. I repeated to myself over and over, *Paula, don't get emotionally involved. You know he's not a Christian.* But my enthusiasm for other guys faded as I saw Curt more frequently.

CURT: At that time, I wasn't in touch with my emotions enough to know how I felt about Paula. I didn't feel comfortable around people, and I would usually let her lead the way in talking or in making decisions. She had frizzy brown hair and laughed easily in a rolling, high-pitched voice. Where I felt clumsy in conversation, she was smooth and easy-going. She relaxed me.

We grew closer the remaining weeks of the summer. Being with Paula solved my loneliness.

When the summer ended, though, and it was time for me to head back to school, I automatically assumed it was time to end what we had going. Being a student a hundred miles from a girl wouldn't work. She would interfere too much.

The week before I left, we sat together under a big oak tree. The summer had been abnormally hot, but a cool breeze made that day delightful. I'm sure Paula expected something very romantic. Instead, I said, "Well, it was a really nice summer,

Paula, but I guess we won't be seeing each other any more." I was fighting hard to keep the relationship from breaking through to where it would really affect me and get out of my conscious control. I was unprepared for her reaction.

PAULA: I got MAD! I cried and cried and struck out at Curt. "You can't do this to me!" I said. "I won't let you—you mean too much to me for that." We talked the rest of that afternoon—under the tree, walking through town, in Curt's apartment. His defenses never cracked, and I saw I couldn't pierce through to get to the real emotions inside. After a long, draining afternoon, I resigned myself to losing Curt and said, "Well, Curt, at least please don't forget the things we talked about . . . about becoming a Christian." He promised.

Months before, I had made a covenant with God that I wouldn't marry Curt, but my emotions betrayed me. They had trapped me. I couldn't forget him. I couldn't put him in perspective. It was like I was possessed with greed or some force which made me *have* to claim him for myself.

His strange reactions infuriated me and puzzled me. But I was too blinded to ever stop and ask myself, "Does this say something about him? Maybe he's not the type of person you should spend your life with. Maybe he's not sensitive enough to you. Maybe it wouldn't work out anyway." Those thoughts never occurred to me. The toboggan ride had started and there was no getting off.

I cried and hurt until I was sapped of all strength, and then I slept for 15 hours straight.

CURT: But our romance didn't end when I returned to school. We managed to see each other at least once a month, taking a bus and train between Chicago and Madison, Wisconsin.

When Paula came, she'd stay in my house with four other college guys. It gave me a certain prestige to have a girl visit me at school. The other guys liked her, because she'd fix meals for us all and straighten up around the house. I began to see some advantages to being married. Sexually, we were getting more involved in making out, but both of us were too scared to go further.

At night, Paula would sleep in my bed, while I slept on a

couch in the same room. It was very strange, sleeping in the same room with a girl. I felt much closer to her, even though we never slept together. She was so nervous the first night she had to get up at 3 A.M. and vomit. I can understand now the guilt she must have gone through.

The biggest thing, the turning point in our relationship, happened unexpectedly in March, when Paula invited me to a weekend of skiing in northern Wisconsin. The camp was nearly empty that weekend. One couple lived there in a trailer. Paula stayed with them and I slept in a second trailer. We had the run of a huge lodge, complete with rustic fireplace. The setting was ideally romantic. In the midst of rolling hills, the camp was surrounded by snow-laced hardwoods and emerald-green pine trees. A frozen lake offered ice skating and crosscountry skiing. Nearest towns were five miles away, and the camp itself included 360 acres of forest.

We would awaken to softly falling snow, gleefully follow the deer tracks outside the lodge, and spend the day skiing and inner-tubing down the slopes.

Saturday evening, our last night at the camp, Paula and I were alone in the trailer. She began to cry as she talked once more about my becoming a Christian. She had become increasingly emotional about it, and I tolerated her witnessing with some impatience. I knew she was probably right, but I had not been quite ready to take such a serious step. Without her knowing it, I had studied the Bible on my own and had gradually learned to believe Jesus really was God. The part about him being alive today and living inside people and the strange things like praying were still foreign and mysterious to me, though.

I had my arm around her. She cuddled close to me and wiped her eyes.

Outside the snow was falling more heavily. Everything was dark and cold but the two rectangular, aluminum trailers—the only spots of light and warmth for miles. I felt very strange.

Finally she asked me point-blank, "Curt, don't you want to become a Christian?"

I was silent for several minutes. There were no sounds but our breathing and the faint clacking sound of the heater fan. Then I said yes.

We prayed together that night. I knew what to say. I asked

Jesus to forgive me for sinning and invited him to take over my life.

My first action as a Christian was to reach over and kiss Paula.

PAULA: Sitting with Curt's arms around me as he became a new person was an incredible, indescribable experience. As he prayed his first real prayer to God, fireworks exploded inside me. Tension had been building for almost a year now. I had made a vow to God not to marry him. I wanted desperately not to fall in love, but I had been unable to stop the process. Now all the tension burst at once. It was like a dam breaking. I felt such a sudden release. How could life be so good! God was too kind, too loving to me! I never dreamed I would have a true, holy love for Curt, without that constant, grating threat of his not becoming a Christian.

Perhaps I had badgered Curt into becoming a Christian, but he meant it. His life changed from that minute. He said it was "like taking on a new job or moving to a new city. There's so much new to explore; I was overwhelmed with the newness, and the lure of the past faded away."

The winding ride home through the north woods of Wisconsin was pure happiness. Snow was falling harder, almost in blizzard strength, and we would pull over every hour or so at roadside parks to wait for snowplows—and to embrace and kiss. We were so happy.

It was a Sunday, and we stopped at Curt's house for lunch. His four roommates were there, and just before they attacked the meal I fixed, Curt said, "Wait a minute, guys; I'd like to pray." He gave thanks for the food, and his roommates knew immediately Curt had been changed.

I took a late train to Chicago. I was possessed with happiness. I clutched my purse close to my stomach and squeezed it, praying thanks to God over and over.

CURT: My conversion seemed to break a seal that held back any obstacles to our getting married. Emotionally, spiritually, romantically—in every way we were much closer after that weekend in Wisconsin.

By the time summer rolled around I had decided to marry Paula. Emotions were still a mysterious, uncharted course for me, and I didn't trust them. But by now sexual instincts forced me to take a stronger interest in Paula.

I was as awkward in proposing to Paula as I'd been on our first date. In the hallway of her parents' home I stopped her and said, "Paula, it looks like we've been going together for a long time now. Do you think it's about time to get married?" She didn't hesitate a second.

Both of us increasingly felt we were being swept along. We weren't really in control of our relationship. It just surrounded us and kept growing. We were together so much we became highly dependent on each other, and it seemed strange to think of life without Paula. I never stopped and asked myself, "Curt, is this really what I want? Is she the one?"

And so our wedding became just one more link in the growth of our relationship. It was a small church wedding. Paula's father conducted the ceremony, nothing spectacular went wrong, and after thirty minutes of music and words our lives were inexorably bound together.

PAULA: Even before the wedding, though, certain trends had started to surface. I had taken leadership in all the decisions about what kind of wedding to have, how much money to spend, the wedding date—even the details of the honeymoon. When I'd ask Curt his opinion, he'd shrug his shoulders and say that it didn't matter. Then I would choose what I wanted.

Naturally the first few months of marriage were jammed with thousands of decisions: whether to buy or make draperies, how to furnish our apartment, what meals to eat, how much to spend on entertainment, how much company to have. Curt seemed aloof, uninterested in most of those decisions, and I wasn't sensitive enough to catch his attitude as a signal that something was wrong with our communication. Instead I barged ahead, arranging the apartment and our budget and our schedule *my* way. It got so that my life was very little changed from when I had lived as a single person. It was just more complex now, since I was running a home for two persons.

Sometimes I felt like Curt's mother. When he drove, I would gripe at him if he made a wrong turn and insist on going my way. I picked on certain parts of his personality that I didn't like and tried to change them. He wasn't a party-goer, but I tried to force him into that mold to bring him out and make him more like I wanted him to be.

On the other hand, sometimes I related to Curt as a little girl. I would whine and beg to get my own way. Curt didn't think we could afford a TV, but I felt lonely when he was away evenings, so I carried on a running campaign to break his defenses. Eventually I won. I always did. I was winning the arguments, but I was losing Curt.

The first clue something serious was wrong was Curt's absence from home in the evenings. His job required him to take a night or evening shift four weeks out of six, so then we didn't sleep together. But he also enrolled in two evening courses, joined a chess club that occupied him once a week, and found other excuses to stay away.

My insecurity boiled to the surface. I would nag Curt about leaving, have fits of crying whenever he'd shut the door. I'd worry about him all night, imagining a car accident or some disaster at work.

Again and again I'd ask him, "Curt, do you love me?" It amazed me that our romance had faded so quickly after marriage. Almost nothing about our time together was romantic.

CURT: Those words "Do you love me, Curt?" I heard as "You *don't* love me, do you, Curt?" I saw Paula becoming clinging and dependent. It was as if she was so dependent she needed me every minute, and yet when I was with her she wanted desperately to control me. I was threatened, and I sought time away from the apartment as an escape. I didn't like the idea of someone clinging to me. Mostly I responded by withdrawing. When I was home I spent the time reading engineering books and fiddling with electronic circuits. It never occurred to me to take Paula's needs and pleasures into consideration; I was too busy trying to escape her.

I looked at Paula's orneriness as being childish diversion. It was her problem, and she'd have to solve it without me. She was already too much an imposition on me.

I felt badgered and trapped, like an animal in a cage being poked with a stick. If I didn't notice her housework or cooking or something she had made, she'd jump on me. Yet, to notice such things was unnatural for me. I had no spontaneous desire to make Paula happy and take an interest in her.

Naturally, some of our arguments were petty enough to solve. Others were almost scary, forcing me to question our whole marriage. When Paula asked, "Do you love me, Curt?" I would dutifully answer yes, but I began to wonder. There seemed to be a current flowing underneath us, eroding away trust and love. We grew further apart.

Because I did not have spontaneous feelings of love, I began questioning my love for Paula. I was still living under the illusion that love is an irrational emotion that wells up from some inner source. It doesn't have to be worked at or exercised, I thought.

I had walked into marriage expecting a finished house. Instead, I found that much building needed to be done; we were only given the shell. But I had no tools. I didn't know where to begin, and I wasn't at all sure I wanted to. So I withdrew, and appeared to be oblivious to our problems.

The tension was eating at me inside, though. You can't just ignore conflict, not in a situation like marriage where you're rubbing against each other all day. It came out in me in the form of colitis, an intestinal ailment caused by constant tension.

PAULA: While Curt was internalizing our problems, I was becoming desperate. Once, in a heated argument, I actually walked out on him, something I never thought I could do. It was clear to me we needed help. I couldn't cope with the problem, and, like Curt, I had no tools to build with.

A month before our first anniversary, I sat alone one evening and reflected on the first year. I saw a year scarred with brushfires of conflict. And as I considered my predicament, I realized that now I was very little different from before I was married. I relied on single friends for my needs, not Curt. To satisfy my ego and to feel fulfilled, I poured energy into my job. Curt was more a complication than anything else. We had little joy together.

I mentioned my thoughts that night to a friend, who suggested a therapist she went to.

The idea of going to a therapist scared me at first. My image of a person who needed counseling was someone with severe emotional problems, on the verge of being institutionalized. My church background made me distrust psychology in general. I saw all problems as "spiritual" in nature. Admitting a need for counseling help was almost a spiritual defeat—I mean, why wouldn't prayer work?

But in reality, prayer wasn't working for me. It did change my outlook and my emotions, but it didn't help me communicate with Curt.

My first visit with Bob, the therapist, brought one of the most stunning revelations of my life. I had carefully outlined all the problems in our marriage from my viewpoint. I expected to describe those problems to him and get a systematic approach to deal with them.

Bob, however, seemed almost impatient when I talked about "our marriage." He told me bluntly, "Paula, your marriage isn't the problem. Marriage is not a mystical state that can be handled and analyzed and put back together. Marriage is just a word to describe two committed people living together. The problem with your marriage is your own problems with yourself and Curt's problems with himself. Let's talk about those."

What he said made sense, but I had trouble adjusting to the new approach. I guess it was safer to discuss something vague like "marriage," whereas I felt exposed discussing myself.

Bob asked, "Paula, do you act like a little girl to get attention?" My eyes widened. I sat up straight in my chair. How did he know?!! "It's obvious from the prissy way you walk down the hall, Paula," he continued.

That night I began to look at myself in a different light. I needed his perspective in picking out the games I played in getting what I wanted from my husband.

Without telling Curt, I started going in regular weekly sessions to the therapist. I was amazed at his insight. He didn't offer packaged solutions; he simply pulled out of me the tricks and gimmicks I used in relating to other people. Most of them were habitual and performed unconsciously. But I began to see why Curt pulled back from me and felt trapped by me. I had been badgering him and "using" him.

As Bob gently poked holes in my defenses, I would nod my head and realize, "Paula, the game's up now. You can't keep up those tricks. You've got to learn to deal with Curt as an adult."

The prospects were a bit frightening, but the fear was tempered by a new feeling rushing in—the feeling of hope.

CURT: I found out about the therapist by accident: I heard Paula talking over the phone to him. When she told me what had been going on, I felt sheepish. It embarrassed me that our marriage had gotten to the place of needing outside help.

But I did go with Paula to see Bob. We met together for a session; then I asked for time alone with him.

We began regular weekly sessions, sometimes with just Bob, other times with a group of four other couples. The group was accepting, and after initial awkwardness, I felt able to be honest with them. We had a common bond, that, unfortunately, I hadn't found among Christian groups: we all admitted a need for help. In Christian groups, dependence sometimes is seen as a weakness.

The therapy came slowly and sometimes painfully at first. I caught myself wanting to escape, thinking, "Why do we have to deal with all these problems. We never did before. Can't we just let some of them slide by?"

Like Paula, I began to see how my own problems as a person contributed to the problems in our marriage. I had never had a warm interest in people. I was much more comfortable reading a mathematics book than meeting friends. Again, I expected an interest in people to just spring from inside me. I had never considered *cultivating* a love for people. But I learned that my personality demanded the support and perspective of other people.

PAULA: And as we confronted our individual problems, we gradually developed to the place where we could see objectively how we had been relating to each other. Bob often used the Transactional Analysis model in helping us identify trends. Put very simply, that model labels three main ways of relating to people. You can choose the Parent Approach where you give orders, imply guilt in your tone, expect an obedient response, give information in a condescending tone. I did that whenever I mothered Curt, and insisted on making decisions in our house. Usually if a person uses the Parent Approach, the partner will respond by acting like a child. In our case, Curt withdrew and escaped from the problem, much as a child will pout and leave the room when his mother scolds him.

Or, sometimes I would use the Child Approach. I would nag and whine until I got my way. I had used this approach in getting a TV. Curt had said there were firm financial reasons for our not getting one, but I chipped away at him until he finally gave in.

Either way, Parent or Child, we were not growing as a couple. We were warring, taking opposite sides and wearing each other down. Awareness of those trends had a freeing, revolutionary approach on our marriage. The first breakthroughs were sometimes overreactions, often humorous.

For example, because I insisted on having my own way, Curt would always obediently follow my directions when we drove somewhere. At every corner I would say, "Turn here, Curt," or, "I'm sure you're going wrong, Curt. Why don't you listen to me?" He learned to fight off that smothering approach by doing the opposite of what I said. Sometimes we went miles out of our way, but he made his point. He was an adult, capable of getting us to our destination without my interference at every corner. I learned to trust him, to allow him to make decisions.

Sometimes the decisions were wrong ones from my viewpoint. Perhaps I really could have done a better job. But the goal of our marriage was not to avoid mistakes; it was to affirm each other and develop as persons. I learned to give Curt support, even when he made a "wrong" decision, instead of scolding him. I realized that he could be beautiful just in taking leadership and making the decisions.

CURT: Paula's support convinced me that I could make mature decisions. I didn't have to go through an agonizing process of thinking, *Now what will Paula approve? If I make a mistake, I know she'll jump on me, so I might as well predict in advance what she'll like.* I began to think through as an individual how I really felt. Did I want to buy a small house or continue living in an apartment? Did I like the church we attended, or were we going because it was similar to Paula's home church? I found that I could make mature decisions, with Paula's input, but without that constant threat of getting her stamp of approval.

We learned to discuss a decision, with true give-and-take. I would say, "Paula, here's a problem. We need to decide how involved we should be in church. What do you think?" Then, mutually, we could arrive at a decision.

A strange thing happened. I started to love. As I've mentioned, I had conceived of love as a mystical feeling that descends upon people. It's either there or it isn't. Not so. Love grew as I got support from Paula. I began to see she was making serious efforts to help me grow as a person.

I started thinking about ways I could please her. She liked to go out to eat. Previously, I had built up defenses against that: we didn't have the money; I didn't want to dress up; I liked home cooking better. But I began thinking, "This could be a very considerate thing for a working wife. It would relieve the worry of preparing a meal and allow us free, quality time together." A subtle element had crept in: I *wanted* to spend time with her.

And I found that love was personal, almost alive. It *grew*. It enlarged as I became considerate and as I felt affirmed and loved. It was inextricably wound up with the actions of our marriage, not apart from them. It's a simple concept, but I had never grasped it.

PAULA: Christian books on marriage often quote Ephesians 5:24, which says, "Wives, submit yourselves to your husbands." But two verses earlier, Paul said, "Honor Christ by submitting to each other." What does that mean? We became convinced it means to recognize the parameters of allowing each other to be an adult without interfering. Curt's desires and opinions are important in our marriage. And mine are important. Sometimes one of us submits to the other's opinion and does something he would not ordinarily choose.

And sometimes we submit by allowing the other partner the independence he needs to be an adult, without necessarily involving the other partner. For example, I learned to respect Curt's time alone in reading engineering and mathematics books. Perhaps the practice of reading books didn't strengthen our marriage; after all, we weren't spending the time together. But it was an important part of Curt's being an individual, and I had to submit to him and respect that. I couldn't jealously possess every minute of his time.

CURT: I'm sure our marriage will be filled with conflicts and disagreements as long as we live. But we have some tools now to work with. We've learned to communicate by honestly stating how we feel about each other and by learning to submit to each other. And we've realized that marriage problems are really *people* problems. The beautiful thing about marriage is that it can be the best medium for solving people problems. If partners are loving and understanding, they create a tremendously warm environment for growth. If the two are pulling together instead of apart, marriage will never be static. It will grow.

Sometimes we still think we would have been happier married to other people. It may be true. But, as Christians, that's not an option to us any longer. We are committed to each other, and we're going to make it work, with God's help. Our marriage is an adventure. There's no backing out.

WHAT DO YOU THINK ABOUT THE ABBOTTS?

The Myth Exposed

Charlie Shedd begins a book of advice to his about-to-be-married daughter with this sentence, which exactly summarizes the Abbotts' marriage: "Marriage is not so much finding the right person as it is being the right person." [1]

Our culture trains us to look for that "one special person" meant for us. But, if we believe that, after several years of marriage we can wake up and decide that since our partner is obviously *not* that person, therefore the marriage will not work.

Almost every marriage expert scoffs at the notion that you can only have happiness with one person, or even one type of person. Paul Tournier says flatly, "So-called emotional incompatibility is a myth invented by jurists short of arguments in order to plead for a divorce. It is likewise a common excuse people use in order to hide their own failings. I simply do not believe it exists. There are no emotional incompatibilities. There are misunderstandings and mistakes, however, which can be corrected where there is the willingness to do so." [2]

Compatibility is, in fact, a state which married partners

achieve. It is not a quality present from the beginning. When trouble comes, it's easy to blame something as vague as incompatibility: "Oh, we've hit a roadblock because we are incompatible." Actually, the roadblock is an opportunity to demonstrate that you *are* compatible.

Is that concept hard to accept? Reflect on Curt and Paula Abbott. Each had concluded he had married the wrong person, but, after a fresh whiff of insight, they decided, together, to construct a marriage. It worked.

Honeymoon's Over

What surprises mark your marriage? Is your partner turning out differently than you expected? Young husbands and wives usually offer up a uniform series of complaints about their partners. In *Psychological Factors in Marital Happiness*, L. J. Terman reported results of his survey of 792 wives and 792 husbands. Husbands listed these complaints against their wives: nagging, lack of affection, selfishness, inconsiderateness, complains too much, slovenly in appearance, is quick-tempered. Wives' complaints were: selfishness, inconsideration, lack of success, untruthfulness, complains too much, lack of affection, and failure to talk things over.[3]

Do you identify with certain complaints on the list? Almost all of the complaints are the result of basic personality differences. Chances are, evidence of these traits cropped up early in the romance, but the partner overlooked them. Looking back, Curt and Paula could find seeds of all their differences in the early days of their romance; at the time, however, their minds were elsewhere.

The point is, it does no good to bear great feelings of resentment because your partner turned out differently from what you'd thought. Really, that's as much your fault as his in most cases. If you had noticed more closely, you could have predicted the conflict. Are you harboring resentment and blame?

What Do You Expect?

Why can't couples predict adjustments before they get married? We've already seen that their romantic perspectives often blind them. Also, there are adjustments about habits they would not know about before marriage (he tosses and turns at night;

she hangs pantyhose in the bathroom; he throws tools into messy, disorganized drawers). These can usually be worked out by compromise.

The really tough problems of adjustment come when partners have different expectations about marriage. Often Curt and Paula clashed over what each expected from the other. Paula expected Curt to stay home evenings; Curt expected an independent wife, not so clinging. What if a wife is used to big birthday celebrations and elaborate Christmas decorations and the husband isn't? What about a husband who expects a seductive, affectionate wife who will hang on him publicly—what if he finds she's physically aloof? Though hints of these differences appear in courtship, often the huge gulf does not yawn open until after marriage, when you are thrust together for sixteen hours a day, not just when you want to be together.

Thus, the real marital battleground is over what each couple expects. Does the husband expect a wife to forfeit a career to be housewife and mother? Does the wife expect the husband to be a career climber? Does the wife expect the husband to keep a well-running, clean car? Who did you expect to clean the garage? Who is to take initiative in sex?

If your expectations differ, conflict will result. Your partner had long training and many rationales to back up his expectations, just as you did. To work out the problem, you will need understanding and a sense of working together. Possibly, like the Abbotts, you will need outside advice. Talk to other couples. How did they resolve their difficulties? Are your expectations unrealistic? In most of these adjustments, there is no "right" or "wrong" way to carry out your roles. It depends on your needs and your partner's.

Sounds of Silence

Did you notice Curt's use of silence as a defense? Marriage counselors observe a common trend in the husband of withdrawing into silence. He may get absorbed in work, find little stimulation from his wife's conversation, or withdraw as a defense to maintain his independence.

Richard Klemer summarizes some important differences between male and female styles of communication that may help you understand problems in communicating. "Not only do girls talk more than boys, they also talk about different things. Girls are encouraged to talk about people and relationships between people—including their own—and boys are encouraged to talk about mechanical and spatial things. This differential conditioning causes several problems in later life. For one, girls expect their companions—and later their husbands—to be interested in talking about the social relationships to the same degree they are. Men often aren't interested. Moreover, the differential conditioning often creates a situation in which the two sexes have little in common to talk about. It is said that when women are together, they talk about things that interest women, like men and clothes and other women. When men are together they talk about things that interest men, like sports, business, and women. But when men and women are together, they talk about things that don't interest either one of them." [4]

Klemer contends that fear is the greatest inhibitor of communication. Curt Abbott was afraid to talk because he felt his wife was dominating him and seizing areas of leadership he didn't want to relinquish. Do you jump on what your partner says with a "Yes, but—" or a "That's not true!" Does your emotional reaction tend to make your partner keep his deep feelings to himself?

There are two parts to communication—listening and talking. Do you talk freely and consciously, thinking of your partner and his interests as you talk? Do you listen attentively?

Inside Out

Curt and Paula Abbott both felt trapped by each other. Their therapist showed them a way out by emphasizing first that they had to get themselves in order. Their security had to come from inside themselves, or they would be parasites to each other.

Some people marry because they believe they have found someone who *makes* them happy. It never works. Happiness is a part of your personality and must develop within you. A partner can make it easier for you to be happy, but he cannot make you happy.

If people are unhappy, like the Abbotts, they often turn to criticism as a salve, blaming the other. Actually, criticism itself is a sign of personal weakness. David Augsburger says, "We criticize because it does something for us. Something we're not

What if Mark didn't like the emerging person I was becoming? What if my new personality was worse than my old one? I would have no defense then.

CHAPTER TWO

To Accept or to Change

MARK AND CYNTHIA PARSONS

Mark Parsons does not recommend his unorthodox way of deciding on a mate, and yet for him it led to a happy marriage. He met Cynthia, a WAC officer, while he was stationed in Alabama with the Army. A group of Christian officers piled into an army car and set out for Officers' Christian Union. Cynthia, the last to be picked up, squeezed through the car door, and slid onto Mark's lap. Embarrassed, she introduced herself.

Two weeks later they met again, this time in Mark's room. Nearby race riots had closed down Ft. McClelland, and only two girls showed up to join Mark in Bible study. The three valiantly proceeded, discussing their goals and values in life. Sue, the other girl, mentioned the goals of learning Greek and Hebrew and having a good career. Cynthia seemed ashamed to admit her goals were to be a wife and mother and her values were simple ones like love and honesty, but her answers appealed to Mark. He was attracted to her lack of pretension.

Mark rarely makes sudden decisions, and as he remembers: "It wasn't really a decision. I was lying in bed when it struck me that I had met the girl I would marry." The next night he went jogging with Cynthia and shared his thoughts. Here's how the conversation went:

Mark: "I have something to tell you."
Cynthia: "OK."

Mark: "Well, it's kinda important."

Cynthia: "Oh?"

Mark: "Yeh, I never said this to a girl before. . . . You can hit me if you want."

Cynthia: "OK."

Mark: "Well, I think I'm going to marry you. I don't love you yet, but I know I will soon."

[*A long silence.*]

Mark: "Did I hurt you?"

Cynthia was not hurt, merely stunned and confused. Mark had much more explaining to do.

From that night on, their romance marched forward with the sense of destiny of a Beethoven symphony. Mark only had one more week in Alabama before being transferred to Joliet, Illinois, so he saw her as often as possible. Though she didn't respond to his proposal that night, Cynthia was attracted to the confidence of this quiet young officer. He didn't try to impress others with flashiness or brashness. He seemed to have his values sorted through.

CYNTHIA: While Mark was in Joliet I was transferred to Louisiana, and our romance developed through the mails and on weekends every three or four months when Mark would fly down to see me. We both were released from the Army about the same time—over a year later—and Mark encouraged me to move to Boston and rent an apartment, since he would be taking training there. It seemed bold and scary, a single girl moving halfway across the country to follow her lover, but I did it. I took an apartment, and Mark lived with another guy. The happiest and saddest moments of our romance took place among the brick buildings and gray skies of Boston.

The first big problem between us developed when doctors discovered I had a serious stomach ulcer. I had few friends in Boston and no relatives. A hospital room becomes drab and depressing quickly, and I lived for visitors' hours. I needed love and support more than anything, but Mark instead pulled back from me. He seemed distant. He visited me faithfully, but I could tell he was holding something back.

MARK: Whenever Cynthia's ulcer attacks came, I would get depressed. I began to view her as a sickly person. I had visions of her destroying all my plans. I feared having to quit school, get a job and support her illnesses. Was I permanently strapping myself to someone who would be sick all the time? I *wanted* to feel love and empathy, but I couldn't. The specters of how Cynthia's illnesses could affect my life hung too closely over me. I wanted to be cheerful for Cynthia; instead I was gloomy.

CYNTHIA: And even though he wouldn't tell me what was bothering him, I knew it involved my illness. The nature of an ulcer is such that the more you worry about it, the worse it becomes. I got sicker.

MARK: The ulcer wasn't the only issue of contention. Many things about Cynthia which appealed to me because they were different also disturbed me. I wasn't sure how to react to those differences. Should I just accept them? Could I live with them forever? Could I be sure I wanted to spend my life with her?

I can remember walking around the tree-lined sidewalks, talking over these problems with Cynthia. The issues were relatively trivial: "You like chit-chat too much; you're not serious about something important to me; you don't always make sense when you talk; you're not interested in the same things I am." I meant these talks as honest discussions on whether we two were right for each other, but Cynthia saw them differently.

CYNTHIA: Though many of the issues were of the type that all couples struggle through, I took them as personal criticism. Was Mark trying to get me to change? Why couldn't he accept me the way I was? In a way it was a test: I felt that I had to make the changes and measure up to his demands for him to marry me. The situation focused unbearable pressures on me. I lacked the security and love-support of marriage. Engagement was a scary, risky experience for me—I knew I was on trial, yet my very worrying about it assured that I would flunk.

When a problem came up Mark would want to talk about the causes immediately, just like an instant replay on TV. I couldn't talk about it—I would lash out, attacking him personally, anything to avoid the issue. He would bring up the comment I made in anger and ask for an explanation. How could I explain my anger without showing more anger? So I would clamp shut and be silent. Then he'd want to talk about why I was so silent. I felt smothered, hounded, attacked, as if I was in a wind tunnel with hurricane-force winds coming from every direction.

MARK: Yes, I was testing Cynthia. I would even set up situations to see how she would handle them. I would ask specific friends over to dinner to see if we enjoyed the same types of friends. Threatened, Cynthia sometimes could not take the pressure. She would fail, and I would wonder, "Do I really want to marry her? Why aren't things working out?"

The issues I faced in Cynthia were real issues. Should I tie myself to a person whose illnesses could possibly change my career goals? That's worth thinking about. But I was approaching it wrong. I was saying, "For this to be God's will, I need to be convinced she and I are perfectly compatible before marrying her." I did not see that if it was God's will, he would supply the strength and courage to love her in all circumstances.

CYNTHIA: Mark was having an enormous impact on me. I respected him as the finest Christian I had ever known. And so when he criticized me, I believed it as absolute truth. He had good judgment, and he never asked something of me which he was not living. But the frustrating thing was, I didn't have his personality and background and Christian life; I had my own.

I wanted to change, and I did feel changes stirring inside me. But I was afraid to let them out. What if Mark didn't like the emerging person I was becoming? What if my new personality was even worse than my old one? I would have no defense then. And so I fell into the old patterns of anger and silence and nervous tension. Because I could sense he didn't trust me, I couldn't trust myself.

My tension passed the breaking point when Mark asked one more test of me. He decided he wasn't ready to marry me that summer as we'd planned. He wanted more schooling in Lansing, Michigan, and he asked me to follow him there, set up my own apartment and give him more time to think about our relationship.

"No!" I said. "That's asking too much. I've already left all my friends and family and followed you a thousand miles from home. I won't do it again! You can't find out everything about me before we get married. You've got to trust me some."

I wouldn't budge. I wouldn't even consider moving to Michigan. I set that up as the one barricade I could not desert.

MARK: Neither of us would give an inch. I was unwilling to take the risk of marriage when I saw certain unresolved conflicts. Cynthia insisted I had to take some risks or she would be beaten down and not worth marrying.

We needed outside help, having reached a dilemma neither of us could solve. I thought of some friends of mine I respected very much. The couple had been Inter-Varsity staff workers, and were good at counseling others. I knew that recently their own marriage had been through tension, so I felt confident they would lead from weakness and understand our predicament.

CYNTHIA: They were Mark's friends, so naturally I was threatened. I assumed they would side with him since they knew him so well. But I had little choice but to see them. Our romance was crumbling, and I could see no other way out. So we called them and set up an evening to drive to their house in the Massachusetts coastal town of Ipswich.

I resented the idea of counseling. I had never seen a good marriage close-hand and I couldn't see how other people could understand us well enough to help us out.

The drive to their home in Ipswich was quiet. Mark and I talked about a few light things, but tension was thick in the car. It was April, and spring was barely stirring in the New England countryside, decorating the bleak and bare scenery. I felt very alone, depressed.

We went for dinner, and the wife had cooked a meal of health food. I remember a soybean-flour cake with peanut butter frosting. They were warm and cordial, and I began to relax. They didn't try to come across as impressive Christian counselors with The Answers; they were fellow pilgrims who had found a few keys for living together.

After dinner we talked in their small, friendly living room. The house was over a hundred years old, and made a very cozy setting.

That evening became a turning point in our relationship. It's not that they told us anything so profound. I'm not sure they told us anything we didn't know already. But they helped us understand each other, overcoming the impasse.

As we talked, we realized that there was much more in common than separated us. We expressed love for each other. The couple agreed with me that I shouldn't move to Michigan. "Mark, you can't find out everything. You can't have her completely analyzed and programed before you're married. That whole project is doomed to failure. You can't make a woman into a man, you can't make a Cynthia into a Mark." And he took it well.

The ride home was an unbelievable contrast. We were full of happiness, and it spilled into conversation. We talked freely, gaily, like new lovers again. Mark pulled off the road, stopped the car said, "I really love you, Cynthia. And I want to marry you in June. Then we'll move to Michigan together." It was beautiful to hear those words. I believed that he did love me and that he finally trusted me.

MARK: Unexpectedly God had to deal with me, not her. I began to see that I really had a twisted, one-sided idea of love. The married couple helped me see that Cynthia's strengths could, in our own marriage or even our engagement, be the most irritating qualities to me. I was too uptight about having all the potential conflicts solved before marrying her. I needed to trust her with some risk. Perhaps I was being too concerned about how she fit in with me.

It didn't take much reading in the Bible to remind me of the true nature of love, that Christ, of course, is the perfect example: "Though He was God, [he] did not demand and cling to His rights as God, but laid aside His mighty power and glory, taking the disguise of the slave and becoming like men" (Phil. 2:6–7, *The Living Bible*). For Jesus, love meant accepting the weakness in others so completely that he was actually murdered for our weaknesses.

The idea of cleansing, forgiving love is one of Christianity's great contributions to marriage. Fortunately, I saw the need for it before I was actually married—otherwise I might have made us both miserable.

Many marriage counselors turn to the passage in Ephesians 5

where Paul lays out his philosophy of how a man and wife should relate. They usually quote verse 25 to the husband: "And you husbands, show the same kind of love to your wives as Christ showed to the church when he died for her."

Naturally Christ wants the church sinless and perfect. But how does he accomplish that? Not by pressuring us and berating us and sternly rebuking us. He is loving and forgiving toward us. He wants our growth, but he refuses to reach in with a magic wand and drive out all imperfections. He allows us the freedom we need to turn to him voluntarily.

My desires for Cynthia's improvement were good desires. I wanted her to be a stronger, more stable person. I wanted her to grow in Christ. But that wouldn't happen if I kept bringing up her weaknesses, wondering if I could accept her personality. To change toward the right, most of all she needed my love and trust.

CYNTHIA: The joy returned to our relationship and the last months of our engagement were happy and filled with love. We were married in Jonesboro, Arkansas, in a ceremony we wrote ourselves. After a two-day honeymoon in Arkansas, we rode a Greyhound bus together to Denver and picked up a U-Haul trailer Mark had rented there. Our first married meals together were graham crackers with peanut butter.

From Denver we drove to Michigan, stopping along the road to sleep out in sleeping bags. (I think it was the fourth night of our marriage when I woke up to a fearsome sight. We had chosen a cow pasture to sleep in, and when I awoke three huge cow heads loomed over me. Their eyes were opened wide, their mouths slightly drooling. We had to chase them away to cook breakfast.)

MARK: From those very first days until now, our marriage has been a blessing to both of us. I really believe it was essential to solve our major problems before we were married. We started out with our commitments and motivations settled. Cynthia never had to worry, "Does he really love me?" She could take that for granted. Our problems after marriage were more adjustments than problems, really. When two people come together, adjustments will take place.

One problem did recur: Cynthia's ulcers. I guess they are a weak spot that affects me. I don't like to see Cynthia in pain. I tend to withdraw and become sullen. Of course she needs the opposite—someone outgoing and cheerful to encourage her. She had several attacks, and it bothered us both.

CYNTHIA: While I worked, Mark continued in school, training to be an engineer. One characteristic I learned about Mark that I had not known was that he needed a few close friends. While we were engaged, a friend of his had come to visit us and it had been a disaster. I resented their closeness and made a scene. I cried and withdrew from them, and they went off to the beach. I couldn't understand how they could be so close and I didn't know how to enter in and make it a three-way relationship. After that, I worked on accepting Mark's friends, trying to enter their mutuality, but also allowing him the freedom to have emotional relationships.

In Lansing the problem intensified because Mark was getting so specialized in the engineering field. I had to learn to force myself to interrupt and ask dumb questions just to stay involved. Otherwise, whole areas of Mark's life would be sealed off from me, and I didn't want that.

MARK: We still practiced different styles of settling arguments, too. I approached most problems analytically and I freely criticized. Cynthia fiercely reacted to anything that could be construed as criticism. She was very sensitive to my putting her down, making her feel like she'd have to "climb to my plateau." She felt unworthy. And I'm glad she did react so strongly; it kept me from mowing her down.

We have learned to compromise on issues where our different temperaments could clash, for example, money. I like a detailed budget which records every cent of expenditure. A newspaper, an ice cream cone, a Bic pen—I want them all written down so I can see the flow of money at a glance.

Cynthia's the opposite. She considers budgeting a tedium that destroys spontaneity. If she has money, she'll spend it; if not, she won't. Why make such a thing over detailed planning?

So we compromised. I roughed out the approximate totals in various areas, say $30 a month for entertainment, $40 for utilities, etc. And I put that amount in envelopes labeled Groceries, Utilities, Books, etc. She has the freedom to spend the money within each envelope, and I have the security of knowing we won't outspend our income.

CYNTHIA: That process of coming together has taken its toll of me. It's hard to accept the fact of being intellectually inferior to Mark. (I still haven't accepted it.) But I have grown to realize my own gifts in working with people. In Bible studies or small groups, I'm the one who picks up on people's needs and can handle problem cases. On Mark's turf—the world of ideas and studies—I'm insecure, but he's helped me to accept my own gifts. I've learned that they are equally important—only different.

I have to fight feeling unworthy. When the ulcer recurs, I feel like a failure as a wife. But Mark has been wonderful in making me feel loved and accepted. I no longer feel the pressure to measure up. In our sex life, for instance, I had problems adjusting because of some bad experiences in childhood. But Mark was loving and understanding. He never gave me the feeling that I owed him something sexually.

We have also kept up the practice of sharing with other Christian couples. People easily seek advice about individual problems, but sometimes avoid seeking advice as a couple. Our experience in Ipswich proved to us the value of counsel.

MARK: When a person sees something he doesn't like, he automatically thinks of how to change it. But a subtle difference has crept into our relationship. I've begun to think of Cynthia's personality in terms of what would be best for her, not what would be best for me. The question in our marriage is not "What kind of wife will please me most?" It's "How can I help Cynthia grow as a person?" and "How can I love my wife as Christ loves the church?" There's a big difference in those two approaches.

Marriage has taught me a rewarding truth about life. You cannot give yourself to another person without helping yourself. Investing time and energy in Cynthia does not rob my dreams and my career plans and my personhood. It enriches me. Love is an investment. And as I give myself to Cynthia, the act ultimately results in my own fulfillment. That's the beauty of love.

WHAT DO YOU THINK ABOUT THE PARSONSES?

Beyond Fear

Mark and Cynthia learned (before marriage in their case) a new depth to the meaning of love. Mark saw that he had been attaching conditions: "I will love you if—" If he had continued with this version of love, his marriage could have been founded on fear and mistrust.

"Real love is not for cynics, pessimists or critical analyzers and worriers. Real love requires being able to see the best—not the worst—in the other person from the beginning. It includes having a reasonable amount of trust and faith that your partner will turn out for the best—after you are sure you could adjust even if he didn't. It demands a kind of courage to put aside your fears of 'what will happen' that often distort the vision of those who have seen too much of life's unpleasantness." [1]

As you read about Mark and Cynthia, whom did you identify with? Does your partner feel totally accepted by you?

Whose Change?

Much marital conflict can be avoided if a partner learns what his mate *cannot* change. For instance, Mark realized Cynthia could not change her anxiety and ulcer condition by concentrating on changing it—that would worsen it. She needed support and affirmation, not lectures. Some people are activists, some are easygoing. Some are supersensitive, some are humorous, some are shy. Before you attempt to change your partner, *be sure the change must be made*. Perhaps the change ought to be made within you: you should learn to accept your partner. Forcing a partner to change is very, very tricky. Do it only in emergencies!

Forget about your spouse for a moment and think about yourself. What do *you* need to change? Certain behavior practices are generally looked on by marriage experts as unhealthy. None of us is totally balanced, and we may have these idiosyncracies to some degree, but they can serve as warning signals for needed self-change.

1. *Do you strongly resist change?* Do you resent suggestions, defend your ways, cling to the status quo? Are you inflexible, haughty, bigoted?

2. *Are you overly systematic?* Some people are slaves to intricate systems of being organized and neat. Although systematizing can be an emotional crutch to you, it may make others uncomfortable and cramp their freedom.

3. *Are you overly sloppy?* Many conflicts could be avoided if a sloppy mate would give a little and accommodate.

4. *Are you overly critical?* You might enjoy it, but those around you will tire quickly. Do you enjoy sarcasm?

5. *Are you known as an inordinate worrier?*

6. *Do you make quick, spontaneous decisions without consulting others or taking all the factors into account?*

7. *Are you a procrastinator?* [2]

The Hate Book

Mark Parsons found to his amazement that, when he stopped bringing up those areas he didn't like about Cynthia, for the first time she began to deal with them. She needed, not lectures, but an assurance that he loved her as she was, in spite of things he didn't like.

Many couples discover this paradoxical human principle: as soon as you stop trying to change someone and accept him, he may well change on his own.

Lionel Whiston relates this classic example: "A wife who was left alone evening after evening started to keep a 'hate book,' making careful note of the time her husband was not at home. She wrote down the exact number of minutes he was with her during her waking hours. He spent only two evenings at home in seven weeks, most often dining out with business associates. His wife recorded it all, waiting for an appropriate time to face him with the devastating statistics.

"Meanwhile, God began to work in her heart. He showed her that she was so bitter that the few minutes she did have with her husband were made doubly unhappy. The thought came to her:

'Why not make those moments together interesting and pleasant?'
So the hate book was thrown into the fire and the brief intervals
with her husband were packed full of love and laughter.

"Within weeks he began to spend more time at home, and
soon afterwards he faced up to the way he had been shortchang-
ing his family. Foundations were laid for a new and more satisfying relationship in the home." [3]

The principle is this. You are responsible for only one partner
in your marriage: *you and only you.* If you're expending energy
worrying about your partner's weaknesses and shortcomings instead of your own—watch out.

Ask yourself, "Do I spend as much time thinking about
whether I'm a good mate as I do thinking about whether my
partner is?"

Change-makers

After all these warnings, I will admit there is a place for one
partner to gently push the other toward behavior changes. After
all, I may never know how irritating one of my idiosyncracies
is until my wife points it out to me. However, if you ever attempt
it, keep these principles in mind:

1. Security is probably the most important environment for
good communications. Work first on making your partner feel
secure. Never, never give the impression that your love or approval is dependent on whether he makes the change you desire.
And never use unfair tactics, like withholding sex, as a bargain-
ing ploy. Those tactics always lead to hurt and sometimes to hate.

2. Affirm your mate, don't possess him. If you can do it without seeming mechanical, it's a good idea to precede each minor
criticism with some praise. (If you ever feel dubious about this
walk-softly approach, spend a few minutes reading 1 Corinthians
13. You may even change your mind about the criticism.)

3. One marriage counselor suggests banning "station-to-
station calls." [4] These are instances when one partner talks to
another as to a public figure, not a loved partner. He assumes a
role, such as teacher to pupil, employer to employee, doctor to
patient or counselor to counselee. (Or parent to child, as other
couples have mentioned.) Cynthia Parsons admits resenting the
feeling that she was one more of Mark's spiritual counseling
targets.

4. Don't neglect your mate's self-esteem. Some people who put on hard, independent fronts seem impervious to criticism. But you can take as a universal rule that everyone is sensitive and will react to criticism. Don't beat down your partner; remember his self-esteem.

Money Methods

The Parsonses worked out an ingenious method for dealing with their money differences. Money can seem trivial, but noted sociologists such as Robert Blood believe that money is the most common source of conflict between husbands and wives. In 1967, in a study by Judson and Mary Landis of three groups of couples, all three groups listed finances either first or second place as a cause of their problems in marriage.[5]

If money is a problem for you, I suggest you find the book *Being Married* by Evelyn Duvall and Reuben Hill. Duvall and Hill list five separate systems of handling money.[6] In the "dole" system, one family member hands out money a little at a time to other family members. The "family treasurer" system differs from the dole in that the treasurer handles the money, but does not control decisions so exclusively. The "division of expenses" system assigns some expenses to the husbands (e.g. rent, car, insurance) and some to the wife. The "joint account" system of having an account accessible to both works well when both members are responsible and the income exceeds expenses. The fifth system, the "budget" system, Duvall and Hill believe to be best for most families. Expenses are agreed on by both parties and budgeted in advance, and excess goes into a common fund that is spent only by common agreement.*

Your pastor should know someone in the church who would gladly help you work out a mutual budgeting program.

---

*Need help on budgeting? Pamphlets are available from the U.S. Department of Agriculture, Home and Garden Bulletin #98, *A Guide to Budgeting for the Young Couple;* and the U.S. Government Printing Office, Education Division, Institute of Life Insurance, *Money Management for the Young Adult,* 1966.

We were trapped in circumstances bigger than we were. Perhaps a strong, optimistic Christian who believes the Christian life is a succession of victories could have made better use of the situation. We could not.

CHAPTER THREE

Trapped in Paraguay

BRIAN AND DIANE REDDICK

In an experiment designed to test the effects of stress, scientists placed a colony of rats in a metal cage and subjected them to a series of mild electric shocks. The rats first acted tense and irritable. They shivered in fear, cowered in the corners of the cage, showed signs of neuroses. But when the electric current was increased, the rats took on a new approach: they attacked each other, biting and clawing. Once outside pressure passed a tolerance threshold, they turned on their closest neighbors.

Anyone in a high-tension situation—for example, a faltering business which is laying off employees, or an infantry battalion under heavy fire—knows the human equivalent of the rats' reaction. When circumstances crack through our defenses, we assess blame and take out our tension on each other.

Marriage can be a pressure cooker. It locks you in with a partner maybe sixteen hours a day, and sometimes twenty-four. Together you face life's tensions, for unless you are very skilled, you cannot hide inner feelings from a discerning mate. And when outside forces converge on you, often your partner takes the brunt of your reaction.

Few couples will undergo an extraordinary sequence of pressures such as were piled upon the Reddicks in a short period. But hopefully, reading about their responses in the face of tightening pressure will better prepare others to face their own tensions.

BRIAN: When we got married, I was convinced I knew everything about Diane. We had gone together for almost six years, and had scarcely spent a day apart during that time. We attended the same private high school, where only twenty-two kids were in our class. We'd sit together in every classroom, share time between classes, and see each other at night and on weekends. We went to the same college and repeated the pattern. I saw Diane ecstatic, hysterical, irritable, nervous, moody, suffering—in every conceivable mood. I went into marriage with open eyes, certain that I knew the person I was marrying.

DIANE: We both wanted to be missionaries, and Brian chose the country of Paraguay because he had visited there on a short-term project in high school. The three months of preparation after our wedding were exciting. We spoke in churches, were invited to peoples' homes for meals, and generally lived under a spotlight. Both of us felt very much in love, and very confident that we were about to embark on a mission that would make even God proud.

We believed we knew each other well enough to skip the two years or so most couples wait before having children. We thought we would enjoy a little baby more if we had one while we were still young. So we did not practice any kind of birth control.

BRIAN: Three months after our June wedding we were in a jet high over North America headed for Paraguay. I could hardly wait to show Diane all the places I had visited there, and to introduce her to the missionaries I had met. After only a day in the beautiful capital city, a missionary met us with a Jeep to take us to our station. The scenery was barren and hilly like the Southwest United States, but to me it was gorgeous. I kept poking Diane and pointing out various landmarks.

Diane was reacting a little differently. We had suspected she was pregnant already, and the Jeep ride and change of climate combined to make her nauseated. The road was a sun-hardened,

two-rut trail marked with bumps and potholes, and she gripped
the door handle with one hand and my knee with the other.
Once, I remember, she poked me and asked, "What are you
getting me into?" I laughed and continued my tour-guide spiel.

Our first eight weeks in Paraguay were spent with several
missionary families on a small ranch which the mission used as
a kind of halfway house for new missionaries. Surrounded by
other Americans, the culture shock was not pronounced, and we
had time to adjust. We soon found, though, that the missionaries
were a hard group to get to know. They could not empathize
with our wide-eyed ignorance. Many things they took for granted
—post office regulations, the banking setup, buying at the
market—were brand new to us.

DIANE: I clung tightly to Brian those first eight weeks. Since he
knew some of the missionaries, he could at least chat cordially
with them. It frightened me to walk to the village and hear in-
cessant chatter in Spanish. The open markets turned my stomach,
they were so unsanitary and fly-populated. During those eight
weeks I stayed near the compound, fighting off morning sickness
and trying to learn basic Spanish words. A doctor confirmed that
I was pregnant, and that excited us both. The other missionaries
seemed to enjoy telling me scary stories about having their first
child in a foreign country.

When our two months at the compound was up, the mission
found a house for us on the edge of a small town of about 5,000.
They insisted we needed to mix with the nationals, learn the
language, and absorb customs on our own. Anxious to be good
missionaries, we moved with eager anticipation.

BRIAN: I'm not sure I would call Diane's reaction "eager anticipation." As I remember it, I was the only one who felt a sense
of adventure and excitement. Diane was desperately homesick
for her family. I had to force her to go to the town and meet any
Paraguayans. But mostly she was preoccupied with complications
in her pregnancy, such as a kidney infection. Seeing her pregnant
brought out all my protective instincts, and I let her stay sheltered.

By rural Paraguayan standards, our house was modern and

well-equipped, but it would not have passed a building code inspection in America. The walls were thin plaster, the roof leaked when it rained, and we had no hot water. We did have cold running water, though, an unusual luxury.

DIANE: In December came our first hint that twins could be on the way. One doctor suspected it, but the fact was never confirmed until a week before they were born in March. I am a very small person, and they anticipated labor could be very rough. It took seventeen hours of hard labor to deliver, which left me completely exhausted.

In the delivery room, I was trying to concentrate on all the correct breathing exercises I'd learned, while the doctor shouted orders to me in Spanish. I felt very alone and alien. Everyone around me was dark-skinned and speaking a different language. I didn't sense any concern coming from them. If Brian hadn't been in the delivery room, I'm not sure how I could have done it.

The twins were born twenty minutes apart—both were boys. The very next day, as is Paraguayan custom, I was sent home from the hospital with the boys.

BRIAN: Our life changed drastically after that. Diane came home weak and sickly and too tired to care for herself. We had no experience in raising babies. The boys were a few weeks early, so they needed frequent feedings. Every two hours we had to get up, and I'd feed Joe while Diane would feed Steven. We never got more than a couple hours of sleep at one time. We were tense and irritable.

I have a vague, dreamlike memory of those months: walking around in a zombielike trance, rocking a baby, coaxing him to take a bottle, listening to Diane's instructions, changing diapers, washing in make-do facilities, trying to keep everything clean and sterile.

All my language work ground to a halt. I couldn't even leave the house; something might happen to the twins and Diane would be alone. Even if she yelled for help and a neighbor came, they couldn't communicate.

After two months I had to leave town to pick up our baggage on the coast. It had been misrouted to another country, and missed our arrival by seven months. Packed in the steel barrels were all Diane's maternity clothes and all the overdue essentials such as diapers and bottles.

DIANE: I have never felt so lost as I did the week Brian was away picking up our baggage. I couldn't keep up with all the chores. I spent most of the time crying and fantasizing what it would be like to have twins back in the States. There, my parents and Brian's parents would be ecstatic, and I'd have no problem getting help with the work.

I was delighted to see Brian when he returned with our baggage, but soon our relationship slipped back into the old rut of irritation and quarreling. I can see now that the problem was one of not meeting each other's needs. You love someone when he meets your needs and in turn you want to meet his. We didn't even have time to think about each other. I seldom felt like having sex with Brian. He resented me for that, but when I did give in he resented my begrudging attitude. He saw me as harried and chained to the house. I'm sure I was no fun to be around. He probably wanted to escape my complaining and griping. But I couldn't help it. Everything was going wrong, and who else could I talk to?

BRIAN: The tension of having to hang around the house all day grated on me. I knew friends and churches back in America were sacrificing to pay our salary, and I couldn't see any mission work getting done. Plus, I was bored stiff. I wanted to go play soccer and meet some of the nationals. Diane would argue, pleading with me not to leave her. Usually I'd go anyway. I knew she had needs I wasn't meeting, but I finally took a "so what" attitude.

Diane was always too tired. Just taking the kids for a walk downtown was a big hassle. I resented her, and accused her of withdrawing into a shell, afraid to come out and meet people. She felt insecure and unconfident in a strange country; I was adjusting rapidly and saw that she was holding back my growth. Perhaps under other circumstances I would have been more sympathetic to her situation. But I saw her as a burden on me.

Since neither of us felt our needs were being met, we often turned on each other. Any little thing could lead to an argument.

Diane never voiced it directly, but she let me know that she blamed me for "taking me down here and getting me into this mess." Before we left, she had told people that Brian was the one called to the mission field; she was going along as his obedient wife. I didn't see it at the time, but that attitude set up an easy out for her to blame me. She had never fully participated in the decision. She had let me make the decision, agreed with it, then blamed me for it later. That underlying disagreement caused much tension between us. It could not change unless we left Paraguay, and I wasn't about to desert.

DIANE: I was still shy about meeting people. Brian had to go almost every day to buy fresh fruits and vegetables; no baby food was available. I didn't like going to the market.

A maid came in and cooked our noon meal, but that got old fast. She cooked the same meal for two months straight: rice with some stringy meat.

It gnawed at me that I couldn't be a good wife to Brian. My vision of a wife was one who cheerfully helped her husband relax, then set a beautiful candlelit dinner before him every night. After a day with the twins, I could barely muster enough energy to put on soup and sandwiches. We had few appliances, and prepared food was unavailable, so cooking was a mammoth chore. Because of our sparse, wobbly furniture, I never felt my home was something I could take pride in. Being locked in it all day drove up feelings of resentment and anger.

I cried a lot, and complained a lot. I tried speaking the language, but I tired quickly of talking like a little kid. I couldn't express any important thoughts in Spanish.

I lived for the time every day when the postman would arrive, devouring *National Geographic, Reader's Digest, Time*—anything which mentally transported me away from Paraguay.

BRIAN: Some people have the image that missionaries are spiritually superior to other people. I've never felt less spiritual than during those first two years in Paraguay. We would turn to God in anger and cry out, "Lord, we need some relief. We're tired of this rotten routine. We need help!" But nothing would happen, and the next day we'd have to gear up for the same chores.

I felt rotten because I was doing such a lousy missionary job.

I couldn't keep control of my own temper; how could I preach to others? I had read books like *Hudson Taylor's Spiritual Secret,* and they made me feel worse. I had no spiritual secrets. I felt miserable. Usually I blamed it on Diane and her griping.

Perhaps it would have helped to have had more preparation time in our marriage. We immediately faced massive changes by moving to another culture and adjusting to twins. We skipped the newlywed stage of getting to know each other and setting up basic patterns of relating. Too suddenly we were overwhelmed with the mere process of living, and we did not enjoy life.

I've asked myself, Should we have gotten married so soon? Should we have come to the mission field so soon? Should Diane have gotten pregnant so soon? The resounding answer to all those questions is NO! We robbed ourselves of a crucial incubation period. We were blinded by our own idealizations of married life, and our own immature cockiness that convinced us we knew each other perfectly well.

Diane got no sense of pride and fulfillment in her role as a mother and a wife. I got no pride and fulfillment in my role as a husband and missionary. I'm not sure if that could have changed. We were trapped in circumstances bigger than we were. Perhaps a strong, optimistic Christian who believes the Christian life is a succession of victories could have made better use of the situation. We could not.

Life was so hectic and depressing and tiring that we stopped even turning to God. What was the use?

DIANE: When the twins were almost a year old, we were transferred to a frontier settlement which bordered a large Indian reservation. Brian was asked to take over as youth director of five churches there—four Indian churches and one run by Paraguayan nationals. Just the idea of a change brought a temporary ray of hope. There was a chance for a new start: Brian could feel more fulfilled in his work, and our mood would improve.

The town, San Juan, turned out to be a railroad stop, inhabited by 250 Paraguayans. We had no electricity and no running water. The house we were given was infested with rats, mosquitoes, and tarantulas. At night a wild pig with big tusks would shove through our door and try to sleep under our bed.

We couldn't get rid of him. Every night he'd return, banging around, looking for a new entrance.

BRIAN: My ministry was worse in San Juan. Shortly after we moved we learned the government forbade preaching and proselytizing among the Indians. That knocked out four of my churches. The remaining church was full of problems. I held four Friday night rallies in the course of a month and the total attendance was 1 for all four weeks! Only one girl showed up.

We saw immediately that the place was a disaster, but I didn't think leaving the problem would be a solution. The mission was sensitive to young missionaries who "can't take it."

Our debts began piling up, producing tension in me. We had raised enough support for one couple, but with the combined effects of twins and inflation, we were soon getting even less than minimum for a couple. I had to charge all our food bills at the local grocery, running up bills as high as $500. When our checks came, every three months, the total of $720 would pay off the groceries and give us $220 for everything else. Then I'd start a new round of debts.

I had heard back in America that money problems and debts were the number one cause of divorce among young couples. I began to see why: the debt situation cut into my self-respect, making me feel I was incapable of providing for my family. It limited my freedom. When I went to the store, I could not even afford simple extras like cereals and candy. I began to understand the despairing poverty mentality of the Paraguayans.

Our circumstances ruled our life. Our options were limited by debts, by the twins, by an unfamiliar culture. And our marriage reflected that sensation of our lives being out of control. We felt pushed, swept along.

DIANE: Usually, time allows you to forget despairing feelings. Memory shrinks down bad experiences into a one- or two-minute foggy scene representing many months of turmoil. But I know that there were very few happy moments our first four years on the mission field. We tried things to cheer us up for a while. Then we stopped trying.

We did not turn on each other so severely as to threaten

divorce. Perhaps in America we would have. But in Paraguay, there was no choice. We only had each other; we were banded together against the situation.

In fact, we were together so much, that I think our very familiarity bred problems. Brian did not have a 9 to 5 job, so he was often around the house. When his ministry attempts failed, he would hang around more, and his frustration rubbed off on me. I learned there how important it is to have outside stimulation. It's no good for a couple to be around each other constantly, with no other outlet for emotions, no stimuli to change and to bring freshness to the relationship. We got in each other's way, blaming each other for petty things. Basically, we got tired of each other. I needed him desperately, but I resented him just as desperately.

BRIAN: I think it would have solved some problems if we could have spent time alone, together, away from the pressures. I'm sure it would have worked, because on our first furlough, so many of our problems faded away. But in Paraguay there was no escape. The twins were always crawling around, tearing up food boxes, eating dirt, falling off the steps. We could not relax.

We began with such idealized views of married life and of mission service. We thought married life would be full of visible affection and harmony. We pictured ourselves working together to surmount every problem. Instead, we pulled each other apart.

Perhaps it's better that we stayed on for the full term. I would have had a hard time living with myself if we had dropped out. We did learn some lessons. It was a crash course in handling responsibility and facing crisis.

Now we're back in the United States on our first furlough, and believe it or not, we're raising support to head back to Paraguay.

The furlough has been very healing. We've gotten some perspective on ourselves, and we've gotten some much-needed rest and emotional support. Petty things that used to mushroom into major wars don't bother us at all now. We have time to be together and enjoy each other.

I have learned some lessons about marriage and about the mission field. One thing I learned supremely: there is nothing more important than our relationship. We Christians, especially those of us in Christian work, subsume our marriage to "the Lord's work." Often our family is first to suffer. Well, my family is the Lord's work, and he's given me prime responsibility for it.

I will not allow us to be victimized by circumstances again. I've set certain principles I will insist on. Mainly I've decided that we are important. I plan to raise enough money to keep us out of debt, figuring in inflation for our entire term. Otherwise, I won't go back. I also plan to raise enough to afford a car, so that we'll have transportation and won't be trapped in the middle of nowhere. And I will insist on living in a town where my kids can go to school near us, and where we'll be close to shopping and various diversions.

It may sound unspiritual to other missionaries to insist on certain personal rights. And maybe it points up a weakness in me. But I know I didn't do the Lord any good out there on the first term, and I don't plan to repeat those mistakes.

WHAT DO YOU THINK ABOUT THE REDDICKS?

The By-product

Diane Reddick pinpointed the cause of her marriage's decline when she said, "We weren't meeting each other's needs." If a couple does meet each other's needs, love will result. Love is often the by-product of need-meeting; a person appeals to you initially because he is meeting some need in you.

Very few will face the extreme pressures of the Reddicks' situation. But if you are feeling general listlessness, boredom, unhappiness or dissatisfaction, it often helps to make an emotional checklist of your needs.

Dorothy Baruch describes the basic emotional foods we all crave: "We need love in good measure, and we need to give it. We need to feel that we are wanted and belong. We need to feel that we are capable of adequate achievement so that we can manage to meet life's demands. We need recognition for what we achieve. We need to know that the pleasure which our senses and our body can bring us is permissible and good and that our enjoyment does not make us 'bad.' We need to feel accepted and understood. And finally we need to feel worthwhile and essentially worthy in being uniquely the self that we are." [1]

First, go back through the chapter and try to find specific instances in which Brian and Diane were failing to meet needs. How could it have been different? Think of your own partner. What needs has your partner expressed to you recently and what needs have come through in nonverbal ways? Does your relationship give your partner feelings of strength and value or feelings of rejection?

As human beings, we have to have these needs fulfilled. If a marriage partner fails to sense them and adequately fill them, often the mate will look elsewhere: perhaps a job, adultery, withdrawal, or other friends.

"Do Plans"

Several times Brian and Diane Reddick expressed the sensation that they were trapped in circumstances too heavy for them which they could not change.

When you are overwhelmed by large problems which seem unsurmountable, one key to changing behavior is to choose a specific, workable plan. Some psychologists call it a "Do Plan." [2] It's easier to try one small change in attitude at a time.

For example, perhaps a wife has a problem with a grouchy husband: he comes home every day with a headache and a cloud of anxiety because of problems at work. It would be unrealistic for her to say, "My plan is to make my husband happy every day when he comes home." It would probably be unrealistic to say "I will always greet him cheerfully, in a positive mood." But she can choose specific behavior, such as "I will greet him with a smile and a kiss." Just accomplishing that small change can encourage the wife and perhaps have a positive effect on the husband. It's much easier to greet a smile and a kiss than a frowning, angry wife.

David Augsburger suggests an ancient remedy for a person up against a wall, unable to change.[3] He reminds us of the prayer of St. Francis of Assisi:

> God grant me the serenity
> To accept the things I cannot change,

> The courage to change the things I can,
> And the wisdom to know the difference.

Augsburger suggests drawing two columns and listing the things you cannot change and the things you can. For example, the Reddicks' column might look like this:

I Cannot Change	I Can Change
My marriage partner	My use of money
The fact of two sons	My lousy attitude
Paraguay's inflation rate	My not having devotions

Brian Reddick went through just such a mental process before deciding to return to Paraguay. He determined that his return was conditional on these changes: more money, living in a town, having a car. By doing so, Brian became, not a victim of his circumstances, but the master of them.

A family that constantly feels like a victim of circumstances usually does not grow; they only pity themselves. That's why it's important to make small changes; to reaffirm to yourself that you are in control, you are free, and you can act even though the pressures around you are weighty. The heroes of history are not men who have lived easy, sheltered lives, but men who have stood up and acted despite adversity. (Think of the impact of Alexander Solzhenitsyn in our time.)

Robbed of Incubation

Every young couple will have to endure crises. Serious problems arise when, as in the Reddicks' case, the crises consume all your attention. A strong couple finds a way to make the *relationship* more important than the crises. Here are some common crises young couples must face: money problems, sex adjustments, job pressures, decisions on careers, in-law problems, having children, difficulty in finding friends.

The important question: when you're in the middle of one of these crises, do you forget about your relationship and concentrate only on the crisis? Remember, your mate also has pressing *personal* needs when you are facing outside pressures together. Do you remember to give support and affirmation?

Brian mentioned being robbed of an incubation period when young couples get to know each other intimately. Are you making full use of that period, or are you, too, caught up in the pressures of life?

The relationship must come first. The stronger the relationship is, the easier it is to solve problems like money, sex, in-law pressures.

Gripe Time

Brian and Diane shared a daily rehearsal of gripes. Diane griped about the twins, the primitive conditions, and her fatigue. Brian griped about his sex life, his poor ministry, his finances. Did they really hear each other? Did they go beyond hearing and *empathize* with each other?

Paul Tournier wrote a magnificent little book on true understanding called *To Understand Each Other.* In just 62 pages, he diagnoses the failure most couples have in understanding and communicating. If you feel misunderstood, I strongly recommend you read this book.[4]

Here's a helpful exercise for mature adults who really feel they're being misunderstood by their mates. The next time a recurring conflict comes up, stop. Ask your partner to switch roles for a minute. You articulate what you think his position is; then ask him to articulate why you've been arguing so strongly. It's a good check to see if you are really communicating and empathizing with one another.

If Only

In his book *Games People Play,* Eric Berne mentioned the "If it weren't for—" game. People often shrug off their own responsibility for failure and depression by saying, "If it weren't for those education debts we have to pay off," or "If it weren't for those moods you have" or "If it weren't for a jealous boss—" The Reddicks admit playing "If it weren't for—" games, only they really believe their situation forced them to have a lousy five years. Do you agree with them? Do you play this game?

*It would be easiest for us to kiss goodnight
and dive into bed. But we've found it's
important to get to know each other
again . . . right then, late at night.*

CHAPTER FOUR

Keeping the Rules

STEVE AND JODY GILBERTSON

One of the freshest outlooks on marriage I've come across is
expressed in a book (*Sexual Intimacy*) by Andrew Greely. Greely
says we approach marriage defensively. Take the word "fidelity"
for instance, he says. When asked "Is your spouse faithful to
you?" we hear that as "Has your spouse cheated on you?" We've
substituted negative meanings for positive meanings. We approach marriage defensively, hoping it will survive rather than
finding creative ways for marriage to grow.

Greely said the goal of true fidelity should be a creative frontier of marriage. Each partner should commit himself to be absolutely faithful to the other. He should be faithful to the other's
physical needs by becoming an exciting sex partner. He should
be faithful mentally by being intellectually challenging. Fidelity
means concentrating on how to meet the other's needs in every
area of life.

It's a good concept, one you see fleshed out in too few marriages. Rather than working to meld together, couples tend to
draw lines between each other: *OK, you can demand this much
of me but no more. I've got to maintain my independence too.*

Of all the couples I talked to, Steve and Jody Gilbertson best
exemplify the concept of fidelity in the terms of Andrew Greely.

Though still young and growing, their marriage shows a solidness and maturity. It's a marriage which works, and everyone around them recognizes it.

Some would say of Steve and Jody, "Of course their marriage works. Look at them: Steve is bright, made good grades in school, feels comfortable with himself and with other people. He's outgoing, humorous, friendly. And Jody—she could be a model—tall, slim, long hair, beautiful features. And look at their families: both had loving, warm families which nurtured their self-images and freed them of the hangups many kids develop.

"I used to feel guilty coming from such a good background, and having a life which seems so comfortable," Steve says. "I'm a social worker, and I counsel people with miserable, pain-filled lives. They look as though someone has beaten them every day of their lives. Those who grow as persons do so painfully. But I've come to believe that conflict and pain are not the only ways to grow. A marriage only has so much energy. I can use that energy in discovering Jody through brushfires of conflict and argument. Or, I can use it in positive ways of building bridges between us. For us, at least, the concept of fidelity has worked."

Steve and Jody's marriage operates according to a set of principles they worked out their first few years together. To some, running a marriage by principles may seem cold and sterile. But those who know the Gilbertsons see the warmth and growth which characterizes life. They have merely found their own way to grow together. And their principles are so well thought through I believe any reflective couple can be helped by considering the Gilbertsons.

STEVE: Before our marriage, when we were still exploring and testing each other, our relationship was marked by conflict. We had a special room in college, the lounge in the Music Building, where we would go to work things out. No one ever used the lounge, and we would sit on the overstuffed couch, listening to the sounds of flutes and pianos and violins emanating from practice rooms. Amidst the musical discord we would argue. I'm sure Jody shed more tears in that room than she has anywhere else in her life.

We determined then that our marriage would be different. We needed that painful time of coming together, but we wanted our home to be marked with love, not pain. And so even before the wedding ceremony we were already agreeing to certain principles that would help us live together and love it.

The most difficult and challenging task in our relationship has been to apply these principles consistently, daily. Fidelity principles don't come naturally or flow out of a reservoir of love, just as the fruits of the Spirit in the Christian life don't spring up unannounced. They take work. It's a daily challenge for us, and probably consumes at least as much energy as if our marriage was fueled by the conflict method.

JODY: One of the first principles we agreed on was the principle of *reintroduction*. Have you ever been around couples where the wife and husband seem to live in different worlds? I know some men whose close colleagues at work know them much better than their wives do. Drifting apart occurs especially when a wife stays home and raises children while her husband takes a specialized job or goes after an advanced degree. Gradually their lives develop so differently that they move in two different worlds. After watching that trend pop up in several couples, we decided that we didn't want it in our marriage.

In some way, we are stretching and changing every day. I teach as an aide in a high school, and each new day molds my ideas and my personality. Steve counsels clients and goes to school, and his mind is changing all the time. Because we're busy, it would be natural for that individual growth to push us further and further apart. But we've agreed to make it a point to introduce ourselves to each other every day. We tell each other how we've changed and what we've learned each day.

Sometimes this principle becomes demanding. For instance, there's one day when Steve leaves the house for school in the morning, travels downtown, then works as a county counselor till ten o'clock at night. It would be easiest for us to kiss goodnight and dive into bed. But we've found it important to get to know each other again—right then, late at night. With Steve's day being so full, he's probably changed as a person more during that day than any other. And so we have a ritual: we go out for coffee and dessert and talk over all that happened. I love it, even though I may wake up tired the next morning. I feel I'm a part of his growing process—he never leaves me in the dust.

STEVE: One night I was called out to deal with a crisis. After attempting suicide, a young girl had turned violent. We pled with her, tried every trick to get her to come out of her house and seek psychiatric help. Finally we had to remove her by force and hospitalize her. I was emotionally drained. It was my first experience like that, and I got home after one o'clock in the morning. Jody had already slept some, but she got up, fixed tea, and talked to me until I unwound. I needed that time to calm down and relax. I needed her love then.

As we looked around at young married couples, we noticed that schedules could drive people apart. One friend works in a factory and has to get up at 5:30 A.M. to make it there on time. His wife sleeps until 7:00 A.M. or so, and doesn't see him in the morning. That may be OK for them, but we thought gaps would open between us if that happened in our home. So, though my first class is at 9 o'clock, I get up with Jody at 6. While she's dressing I make breakfast and then we eat together.

It's a simple breakfast: grapefruit (she's trained me to cut the edges to make it easier to eat), a muffin, hot cereal, and tea. Sometimes, after she leaves, I jump back in bed. But it's a time for us to begin the day together, symbolically demonstrating to each other that we're close and we want to be involved in the other's life. You can always make up lost sleep; a slipping marriage is harder to recover.

JODY: The breakfast is nice and builds security. But usually, we're groggy and not too alert, so we've found that the conclusion of the day is the one crucial time we need to reintroduce ourselves. We always spend at least an hour together. Sometimes we go for walks, talking, winding down. Sometimes we sit in bed and talk, sometimes we sing together (Steve plays the guitar and we both love singing.) Or, we may sit in front of a fire and relax together. But that time is sacred; almost nothing can steal it away from us. We're jealous of those moments.

Before you're married, it seems spontaneous fun happens so naturally. During Pennsylvania winters we would chase each other around the block, goose-stepping through the snow. We would make snow angels into deep drifts, spreading our arms and falling stiffly backwards with a soft thump. It seemed nothing was more important than having fun together.

Marriage brings with it time-devouring complications. We have to carefully carve out those fun times. And we need them.

STEVE: Many couples we know get hung up on the problem of who does what in the house. Does the wife do all the cooking? Does she also clean house? What if she works, does she still do the cleaning? Who takes out the garbage? Who gets the car repaired?

As soon as you pull in the driveway after your honeymoon those questions spring up. Somebody has to fix that first meal and do those dishes, and because we live in America most of that work usually falls to the wife.

With the women's movement and our changing society, those issues can cause much conflict. We saw that happening the first few months of our marriage. Our roles and chores started cementing simply because we became used to them so soon. We never thought about it.

JODY: Inevitably, irritations set in. I had certain ideals from my mother about what a wife should be, and I thought I failed if I couldn't match those ideals. The first holiday we spent at home was a disaster. I decided to make a turkey. I was upstairs, dressing leisurely, enjoying the relaxed holiday, planning just how to do the stuffing and prepare the turkey. I wanted to try some new techniques I had read about. I sauntered downstairs, walked into the kitchen and found a fully dressed and prepared turkey, ready for the oven.

I suppose I should have been thrilled at Steve's help. Instead, I was angry. "Can't I do *anything* alone?" I asked him. "Do you always have to butt in and take over from me?"

Several times we crossed wires like that. I would expect one thing of Steve; he would do another. We enjoyed the freedom of not being locked into traditional roles, where the husband keeps out of housework and cooking, but at the same time, we were always bumping into each other.

We came up with a simple agreement to live by the principle of *convenience*. Our chores wouldn't be determined by gender or rigid roles, they would be determined by who had the time. For instance, Steve is a terrible typist, and it takes him twice as long to type a school paper as it does to write it. So I took over the job of typing his papers. There was no argument or resentment. This solution was only natural, and we both accepted it gladly. After all, we're together to help each other, not to compete.

STEVE: My getting breakfast for Jody falls under this same principle of choosing what's convenient. Since I don't have to be anywhere early, I am the one for whom the chore is more convenient. And, since I'm up, I wash the breakfast dishes after we're done to get them out of the way.

We do our cleaning together, usually making it a team duty. And when we have company we share host duties. We'll switch off preparing things in the kitchen and being with our company.

It seems silly to dress this up and call it a principle, but it's amazing what serious problems can develop from such minor things as who does what in a house. We have friends who feel locked into their sex roles. The husband wouldn't dare touch the kitchen garbage or pick up a dishrag. The wife would not consider dropping the car off at a garage or removing a storm window. As a result, they're often irritated because things don't get done around the house.

Marriage should mean freedom and wanting to help, not a bartering of IOU's to make sure each partner does exactly the same amount of work.

JODY: Probably the most important principle we use in guiding our marriage is the principle of *dialogue*. This principle is often the key to whether a marriage will work or not. Watch TV comedies, especially parodies like Archie Bunker, and you see the American stereotype of the lack of communication in families. Archie is boorish, insensitive, not honest about his feelings. In response, Edith looks for ways to sneak around her husband and uses tricks to cajole a decision out of him.

Patterns like that can develop effortlessly. In our relationship, Steve is clearly the more verbal. He approaches people more relaxedly, he carries social conversation and tends to talk the most in our relationship. That's rare; usually the wife is the more verbal. When we argue, something inside at times makes me want to close up and not really share myself with him. I can't articulate as well as he, and I'm not as self-confident.

But that's no good. We'll grow apart, not together, if I shut myself off from him. So I've forced myself to open up to him and tell him what's bugging me even though I don't feel like it. It's easier to keep silent, but I can't. Not if our marriage is to grow. I have to open up.

STEVE: On the other hand, I have to work on my listening skills. I've been around many husbands who barely listen to their wives as they read the paper or watch the ball game on TV. She'll talk about anything in the world and he'll blindly nod agreement or say "uh huh" without the slightest idea of what she is saying.

I tend to frustrate Jody when she starts sharing with me. I complete sentences for her, fill in details, give her instant analysis like a TV commentator after a President's speech. But she doesn't want my analysis, she wants my attention, and I have to work on listening to her.

As part of this process of talking things out, we are committed to the Bible suggestion "not to let the sun go down upon your wrath." The way it works out, we try to keep the sun from *coming up* on our wrath, for we often sit up hashing out disagreements till three or four in the morning.

Sticking to this rule has made a big difference in our relationship. You can spoil yourself by telling your partner you need time to stew and boil inside awhile. Anger can feed on itself and build to almost insane proportions if it isn't vented quickly. We have to get our feelings out and discuss them. We can't wait until the next day or until we have more time—we have to make time that same night.

That agreement keeps us from going inside our shells and sulking for days. I may get really mad, smash my fist against the wall, stalk around grousing all day . . . but when evening comes I know I have to be honest enough to talk about it and work toward a solution.

Some couples have told me, "We can't live like that. We enjoy our anger too much, and anyway we think it's wrong to impose rules on your feelings like that. You're not letting true feelings escape." I ask them, "Oh, you don't have any rules in your fighting? Do you get violent? Do you beat each other?" Everybody has rules, and we're not saying ours are the best. We just know that we've got the potential for severely hurting each other emotionally and it helps to agree to restraints which set limits on ourselves. We protect ourselves that way.

JODY: When two people live together all the time, it produces unique tensions. You turn on each other, insult each other, nag. I nag Steve about his weight when he gains a few pounds. He may jest about my cooking when we have company and I'll recoil. We've just decided it's no good to let those hurts fester inside. We've got to bring them out in front of the only person who can deal with them—the person who caused them.

I have often felt that Steve needs to exert more spiritual leadership. I want him to take the lead in praying and getting us involved in Bible studies with other couples. But it's no good for me to brood on that and resent him. I force myself to tell him and talk over the situation. Otherwise we'll never come to solutions. Only after we both discuss where we're at can we work out a better solution.

STEVE: The area of sexual needs has been the hardest in which to open up and tell each other what we feel. I second-guess Jody or blame her for not meeting my needs, when actually the problem is that I haven't expressed my needs to her.

Much of sexual communication is nonverbal. A slight touch or caress will signal my desire. But if I expect too much from Jody in receiving that signal, I set her up for sure failure and rejection.

One of the great discoveries of my marriage was that Jody is turned-on. She enjoys sex, and she's very expressive about letting me know that. My dad told me to avoid "Christian sex" in marriage. It's tragic that when I use a phrase like "Christian sex" I'm referring to uptight, inhibited sex, because I don't think that's what God had in mind at all. He invented a no-holds barred, exhilarating exultation. He gave us a good example of how it should be in the Song of Solomon, and we go around strait-jacketing it. I want our sex life to be free, experimenting discovery.

JODY: When one partner is uptight about his sexual needs, he really only harms himself. Often we've lain in bed, side-by-side, wanting to make love. But we'll both be thinking, "No, it's almost midnight, we have to get up tomorrow, we're probably too tired." As a result we miss out on the intimate joy and spontaneity that sex can become. Sex is a powerful way to pull two people together: we need to let it do that.

My biggest hangup is that I sometimes feel unappealing. If I get a few pimples, or I'm angry about picking up two or three pounds, I start deprecating myself and thinking *Steve doesn't want me like this.* I have to learn to trust what he says, that he does desire me sexually. I have to accept that, take it for granted.

STEVE: When we first got married, we realized that we could get so tangled up in trying to be secure—personally, financially, socially—that our lives could become flat and boring. That easily happens to young couples. They live close to parents and depend on them for support. They take the traditional sex roles in marriage, without really thinking it through. For some this may be the best course, but we both feel a deep-seated need to keep expanding.

Therefore we've come up with a principle of *risk*. We have determined to push each other to take risks and grow, even though it may not be the most secure option.

Shortly after our marriage we had the chance to be dorm parents to a bunch of college guys. Our first response was no, it would be too threatening to a young marriage. But as we thought about it, we realized we were depriving ourselves of an opportunity to grow as a couple. In that situation we would have to lean on each other and come together. We would learn how to relax around other people; for one thing, there's very little privacy as a dorm parent. The guys had a mock basketball goal attached to a wall, and our bedroom was on the other side of the wall. We could hear them pounding and yelling; they could hear us talking or arguing.

We took the job, and it was a growth year for us. We learned how to handle crisis situations. We learned to be leaders and to let others depend on us. We learned how to maintain order. But most of all, we were in it together, and we needed each other to work out problems when they came up. We had the same job; it was easy to support each other.

We took the assignment for only a year, as we'd planned. But now we're grateful for that year.

I face another issue which demands risk, the same question
many husbands are facing now: how do I feel about my wife's
carrying on a career? My family was so healthy that I've always
dreamed of having my own large, close-knit family with children.
I catch myself wondering if Jody should quit teaching, start a
family, and concentrate on being a wife and mother.

But no, I've got to take the risk of allowing her freedom. She
may need a career for her self-development. She may be totally
frustrated stuck in a house all day with young kids. I can't impose a role on her which she may not want. I have to keep telling
myself—whose marriage is this? Mine or *ours?* I am not her
master or her director, I am her partner, and I am committed to
her growth as a person.

JODY: Because Steve allows me that freedom, it takes pressure
off me in deciding. Of course, his feelings and dreams will be
an important factor in what I decide. The fact that he expresses
them gently and considerately impresses me more than if he
insisted on his own way. That would just have bred resentment.

I suppose I have taken the most risk in the area of sex. Coming
from a traditional home, I absorbed the feelings that a woman
should be the passive, submitting sexual partner. She should not
initiate sex; she should not be too active; she should serve her
husband. But as I have felt sexual desires and urges, I have
gone ahead and expressed them. Steve has responded well; he's
encouraged me to take sexual risks. It's easy to feel sheepish and
embarrassed about sex. I don't think I could have been so open
without Steve's encouraging, accepting attitude.

STEVE: I suppose all the principles we live by could be bundled
up and included in the one great principle of selflessness. When
the Bible describes love in such passages as 1 Corinthians 13, all
the description points to the principle of selflessness. Marriage
can't run on the basis of "Well, these are my rights, and I must
protect them." It must follow an attitude of "How can I make
this marriage most helpful for my partner?"

I read a lot of psychology, and the modern trend seems to be,
let your feelings hang out. Do what you feel like. If you feel
angry, explode. If you feel selfish, pamper yourself. If you feel
tired, withdraw. Instead of freeing you, that philosophy enslaves

you to your emotions. I can't accept all of that. If we each act only on the basis of our feelings, we jerk apart and resent each other. Instead, we've learned to respond to each other's needs, not just to our own feelings.

I have memories of times when I was tired and irritable and ornery and, in spite of my feelings, chose to reach out to Jody and show her love, putting her desires before mine. Those are my most cherished memories.

I counsel married couples for a city counseling service, and without a doubt the problem that screams out from these couples' conversations is the problem of selfishness. Each partner is convinced he is right: he's been wronged and it's up to the other partner to change.

JODY: In many ways a Christian and a non-Christian couple live in the same territory as Christian couples. Two people living together create inevitable tensions that anyone of any faith will face. The issue of selfishness, however, is the one area where we Christians have an advantage. When we're tied up in knots and at the end of our patience, there is a Person to turn to, a reservoir of strength to draw on. Both Steve and I have learned to seek God's power on our own when we need help in being selfless.

My hardest times often come when Steve is away for an evening. I feel sorry for myself, I start to resent him, and it's easy to start brewing on my own self-pity. I feel trapped with myself. But I've learned to turn to God then, letting him ease out those feelings of selfishness and replace them with his love.

STEVE: Coming from good homes, both of us were hopeful that marriage would be a cocoon of warmth and love. Life is full enough of tensions and pressures. I once read a study in which psychologists measured all the input that the average man took in every day. Every time a man heard bad news (like a murder or tornado or war), they recorded negative input. If his boss praised him, that was chalked up on the positive side. If his boss snapped at him, a mark went on the negative side. They kept results from a sampling of businessmen over time, and eventually came up with the figure that 67 percent of the men's input was negative.

If that is true, the situation becomes unbearable if people get an added dose of the same negative input at home. You're bound to crack. Yes, marriage naturally gravitates toward conflict and tension, but why let it? As I read the Bible, that's not the model we should use. Marriage isn't based on status and competition. It's based on forgiving, forgetting love. Love with no end. Love helped by God's strength.

We're determined that our marriage will be a place for us to lick our wounds and gain strength, not a battleground. In some ways that decision is harder: it presses us to think about our relationships daily and exercise our conviction daily. But it works; we're happy with each other. Our love has grown, we have grown, and we look forward to a long life together. Can we ask for more?

WHAT DO YOU THINK ABOUT THE GILBERTSONS?

Losing the Frills

If I asked, "What is the most important quality in a good marriage?" almost any group would give the same answer: Love. But is it? Why, then, do many couples who are separating say, "I still love you; I just can't get along with you."

A good case could be made that Andrew Greely's concept of fidelity is perhaps the most important quality. The problem with "love" is that the word immediately conjures up images of frilly valentines, mushy poems and warm, furry feelings. We think of love as something that *happens* to us, a spontaneous feeling that may appear one day and vanish the next. That kind of feeling is a shaky basis for marriage.

True love includes the concept of fidelity. Steve and Jody Gilbertson have taken a giant step toward a happy future just by realizing that love is something you *do*. Marriage is one of God's gifts to us, like sex, nature and music. But it takes care and feeding.

A good dose of fidelity—the sheer determination that you won't give up on any area of marriage—can pull you through all the dips when love seems to have disappeared. In his book *Sexual Intimacy*, Greely gives an example of an area in which couples need to practice fidelity. In our culture, he says, the man's sex drive is assumed to be obvious and simple. A wife who sees that her husband has regular ejaculations may think her role as a sex partner is fulfilled. "But in fact, the flesh and the nervous system of a man are as delicate and responsive as they are in a woman. There are an infinite variety of shadings and nuances in what a woman can do to the body of a man. When either partner thinks there is nothing more to be learned, then the commitment to growth and self-transcendence in a genital relationship is in trouble." [1]

Fidelity means never giving up on an area like sex. Infidelity, says Greely, is "giving up on any aspect of a relationship when there are still possibilities remaining." Fidelity commits you to bring out the best in your partner and yourself.

Check yourself: Is fidelity a prominent quality in your marriage? Have you given up on any areas—sexual satisfaction, moodiness, "skeletons in the closet," shared time?

Rule-bound

Did you react against the principles the Gilbertsons live by? Did they seem rigid and unrealistic?

Every marriage operates by rules, some verbal, some non-verbal. Consider these: Husband must kiss wife every day before leaving for work. Wife gets taken out to eat once a week. Both partners consult before making a purchase of over $100. Must have Christmas tree every year. Must visit in-laws at least once a week. Wife acts as letter-writer.

Of course, the rules vary with every couple. But problems occur mainly in two areas. (1) If the rules are nonverbal, they're much easier to break. If, for example, a husband comes home with a $300 stereo receiver when the nonverbal rule is to consult on major purchases . . . watch out. The Gilbertsons have clarified their marriage and eliminated potential conflict by agreeing to a clearly defined set of rules. (2) The rules must be understood and agreed to by both parties. It's no fair berating your partner for breaking a rule he didn't agree to. And it's no fair enlisting in-laws or examples of other couples for moral support to prove your point.

What are the verbal rules in your marriage? The nonverbal rules? Here's a revealing exercise: you make a list, then have your partner make a list. Are they the same? Did any of your partner's rules surprise you?

Be a Probe

The Gilbertsons' principle of reintroduction may seem unnecessary to your marriage. Yet, it's easy to find older couples who seem to live in separate worlds. He buries himself in work, about which she knows nothing. She has close friends he has never met. Daily they change, and yet neither is aware of it.

The playwright Eugene Ionesco caricatured the extreme of this situation in an absurdist play *The Bald Soprano*. An English man and woman find themselves sitting together on the morning train from Manchester to London. The scenery is routine for both of them, so after a period of silence they begin conversing. As they talk, they discover they've been married the same length of time. To the woman's surprise, the man mentions a two-year-old daughter. She, too, has a daughter that age. The greatest secret bursts out when one asks the other's address. They live in the same house. Then they realize: they are husband and wife!

Ionesco's fantasy points to a common trend. Often, slippage seeps in unexpectedly. Steve came home tired after a harried day. If he had climbed right into bed, they might never have shared the day's important events.

How well do you know your partner? Did you learn anything about your partner today? This week? Has your spouse changed in the last month? Have you? Does your partner know that?

A clue: Often partners don't share easily but must be probed. And probing takes a skilled questioner. Interviewers Barbara Walters and Dick Cavett have both written books on asking good questions. The key is to find a question that forces someone to think and dredges up new information. "How are things at the office?" or "How did it go today?" are perfect setups for grunts or one-word answers. Instead, try "What was the most interesting thing that went on today?" "Who bugs you most in your job?" "How did you feel about what the pastor said in church Sunday?"

The Whitecaps

Of all the couples I interviewed, Steve and Jody handle their conflicts most constructively. But they, too, have regular, sometimes angry confrontations. Whenever two persons come together so closely, sparks will fly. Shortly before his son Philip was to be married, Charlie Shedd expressed this constructive conflict graphically, using the analogy of a river. "You would observe that, well upstream, before they united, each river flowed gently along. But right at the point of their union, look out!

"Those two nice streams came at each other like fury. I have actually seen them on days when it was almost frightening to watch. They clashed in a wild commotion of frenzy and confusion. They hurled themselves head-on as if each was determined that the other should end its existence right there.

"Then, as you watched, you could almost see the angry whitecaps pair off, bow in respect to each other, and join forces as if to say, 'Let us get along now. Ahead of us there is something better.'

"Sure enough, on downstream, at some distance, the river swept steadily on once more. It was broader there, more majestic, and it gave you the feeling that something good had been fashioned out of the conflict.

"A good marriage is often like that. When two independent streams of existence come together, there will probably be some dashing of life against life at the juncture. Personalities rush against each other. Preferences clash. Ideas contend for power and habits vie for position. Sometimes, like the waves, they throw up a spray that leaves you breathless and makes you wonder where has the loveliness gone.

"But that's all right. Like the two rivers, what comes out of their struggle may be something deeper, more powerful than what they were on their own." [2]

*When we'd argue, all the pent-up steam
would explode. We'd have violent arguments
over issues as mundane as burnt peas.*

CHAPTER FIVE

An Impasse

CLIFF AND SHARON DOMINY

Cliff Dominy was a product of the turmoil of the Sixties. In college during the days of protests and riots, he was just close enough to the pulse of revolution to be distraught, yet just far enough from the real issues to feel useless. After reading Gandhi, he became a pacifist. The scars of angry blacks and the cries of starving children deeply disturbed him.

After graduating, he went on a VISTA tour to see if a stint with an American Indian tribe might allay his guilt feelings. But in the hot Southwest, amid squalor and poverty, he realized, "I didn't want to spend the next two years of my life digging irrigation ditches." Inside, Cliff felt compassion; he wanted to change the world. But he also knew that he was shy and retiring and felt uncomfortable in leadership. He preferred staying at home reading about the exploits of social crusaders.

Cliff is skinny. His 125 pounds are stretched over a six-foot frame, and all through school he was the butt of skinny jokes, such as, "Do you wear skis when you take a shower to keep from going down the drain?" Ironically, he married a girl who fought extra weight. She was not fat, but chunky enough to worry about it and to assume she'd get a leftover among the guys on campus.

Thinking of Cliff and Sharon's marriage reminds me of a very different couple I know who have endured twenty-five years of difficulty in marriage. Of opposite temperament, they moved overseas unprepared for a new culture and suffered tearing family tragedies. Yet their marriage today exudes open, accepting love. Once the wife told me, "I used to think I loved Jack because of certain things about him—his good looks, his winsome personality, his dedication. But it didn't take long to see through all that. I found out over the years there can be only one reason to make me love him. That reason is *because I want to*. We're together, I believe, because God put us together, and I'm *going* to make it work. I will to love him."

As I contemplated Cliff and Sharon's young marriage, I began to realize they lacked the quality this woman said was the key ingredient. After so long, Cliff and Sharon stopped wanting to love each other. There was no motivation left. They were bored stiff.

Brace yourself: there are no syrupy, happy endings in this chapter, and the style is one of open argument, not resolution of conflict. Yet I believe their discoveries speak loudly to young Christian couples.

CLIFF: I suppose you can find the roots to most of our problems back in our engagement period. It's funny how when you meet up with a problem while you're engaged, you think, "Well, this won't happen when we're married. The pressures of being engaged are the reason. Things'll change."

I went with Sharon for two years before asking her to marry me; then we were engaged a year after that. So it's not like marriage surprised us: we knew each other well. Generally, if a couple floats along without really analyzing themselves, they tend to stay together until a crisis builds up. A security grows with familiarity.

Sex can become the glue that pulls you together in spite of anything else. It fills in all the cracks and the hurts with a pleasant sensation. Both of us were from strict Christian backgrounds and had heard all the raspy threats about what would happen when our "desires" controlled us. But those "desires" never come as clearly labeled monsters. They seemed to creep in as an unavoidable, natural part of growing close. It's almost impossible to go backwards with sex. Either you say "Stop!" or you go forward, experimenting, trying something new.

Gnawing, oppressive guilt accompanied our sexual experimentation. After sermons on God's morality at our church, I would pray and ask God to help me overcome this problem. When Sharon went home for a vacation break, I would thrash it out, determined not to fall back into the same sex traps when she returned. I'd spell out my rationale in letters to her, gear up my self-control, and prepare for a new leaf in our relationship. Then she'd step off the plane, something would snap inside me, and we would be half-undressed, petting heavily in our car in the airport parking lot. I could never get my head straight on that. I knew it was wrong. I couldn't conquer it, and I knew it was pushing us inextricably together.

SHARON: At first I looked upon Cliff as a second-rate choice. His skinniness didn't help his looks, and he always wore ratty clothes: blue jeans, long-sleeved flannel shirts and a dumb-looking beret. He walked around campus in his farmer boots, taking long, loping strides—a pale, thin ghost.

Sometimes I even felt ashamed of Cliff among groups of other girls, when we compared guys. But he had certain things in his favor. I was chubby and I knew I probably couldn't attract one of the really smooth guys on campus. And he was older, lived off campus, and treated me gently.

Cliff's idealism attracted me, yet he was not practical enough. I was reared in a comfortable, middle-class home with good furniture and nice clothes. Cliff owned two shirts and would be content with a pile of straw to lie on. He was furious when we started planning the wedding and found I had ordered china and silver.

"What is this, a trap? What are you trying to trick me into?" he'd yell in his thin, high-pitched voice, and I would burst into tears.

The sex thing bothered me some, but not nearly as much as it bothered Cliff. I never got much pleasure from our heavy petting sessions acted out behind trees on campus or an airport parking lot. Yet, on the other hand, I was flattered by Cliff's interest in my body, and I did nothing to slow him down.

CLIFF: A crisis hit us the year before our marriage, fanning our romance's intensity. Outside pressure forced us together, and from that time on we never considered not getting married.

Sharon was on a trip to Texas when a guy "raped" her. She had met him early in the day. He came to her room and without warning covered her mouth, ripped off her clothes, and attempted rape. It was quick and confusing, but Sharon managed to hold him off and keep him from penetrating her. Emotionally, she was shaken, but alone with a girlfriend in a city far from home, she didn't know what to do. She was afraid to contact the police, having heard stories of police interrogation and ridicule. She successfully blocked the event out of her mind, convinced the rape had not been completed.

Sharon told no one for almost three months—not me, not her parents—no one.

SHARON: I think I had truthfully blocked out the memory. I didn't brood on the experience and it didn't make me wary of all men. I just classed it as one of those unfortunate things which happen to girl tourists. Several months later, back in school, I became nauseated frequently, slept a lot and generally felt terrible. I went for a checkup, completely unsuspecting, and discovered the shocking news that I was pregnant.

When the doctor told me, I felt as if a sledgehammer had hit my chest. I was completely unprepared. No one had ever told me that pregnancy was possible without completing intercourse. I felt guilt and anger and grief and pity, and mostly I felt afraid. How could I tell my parents? How could I tell Cliff? How could I face myself? It wasn't like cheating or lying or something I could shove aside. That baby was inside me, growing, and I couldn't escape it.

My parents reacted with predictable shock and the desire to guard their own reputations. I went home the next weekend and announced to Mother, "I have something awful to tell you." Immediately she guessed. "You're pregnant."

"It's not Cliff," I hastily added, then tried to spill out all my confusion and hurt. Fortunately, the doctor verified I was a virgin, validating my story. My parents made all the decisions, arranging for an abortion in New York without giving me time to sort out my thoughts. My father made plane reservations the next day, and called school telling them I'd be out a week. I thought of the baby and fleetingly considered the rights and wrongs of abortion, but whenever I tried to say something, Mother would say, "Now, Sharon, you just hush up. We'll take care of this." Afraid and fighting guilt, I did let them handle everything.

My father and I flew to New York. It was a strange trip. He never talked about the baby; in fact, he told me he never wanted to discuss it. We spent those days making meaningless small talk, our true thoughts hidden and pushed aside.

The abortion was painless. A needle in my arm kept me drowsy for a day. I bled a little, but in two days we flew home, and I returned to school. It was that quick.

CLIFF: You might think finding out about the rape and the abortion would drive us apart. After all, she'd hidden it from me, and there was plenty of room for distrust. But instead I rallied to her support. We made one monumental mistake, however—we told my parents about it. My dad is a cornerstone in a small-town, fundamentalist church, and his ideas are inflexible. As soon as we told them, they came out with statements like "Well, Cliff, you know that in God's eyes she's married to this Texas fellow, and it would be breaking God's moral law for you to marry her now." Or, even worse, they would say, "Cliff, look me straight in the eye and tell me the truth. Was it you? Was there really someone in Texas involved?"

From then on, every letter contained reasons why I shouldn't go with Sharon. Their attitude actually drove us together. They were so unreasonable that I drew close to Sharon just to spite them.

We were married the next summer. I reasoned, "Well, eventually I'll marry, and it will probably be Sharon, so I might as well go ahead now."

SHARON: We were married in my home church in Seattle, had a delightful honeymoon on the Olympic Peninsula, and moved into a tiny, walk-up apartment. The first year satisfied all my expectations about marriage. We got along beautifully. I worked hard at my housework and took special care with cooking and cleaning. We tackled projects together, covering dark, flowered wallpaper with bright slashes of white, yellow, and black. We nosed around garage sales until we found a musty old couch, a bean-bag chair and a huge braided rug for the living room. It was *our* home. We put our stamp on everything: the furniture, the broken-down TV, the curtains, the paintings on the wall.

We were free. No one could break in on us during our sex. We had all the privacy and togetherness we had ever wanted. For the first year, at least, it looked as though our fears and apprehensions about marriage had been unfounded. The fun of living together surprised us.

CLIFF: I agree the first year was a good year. I was sexually satisfied, without all the haranguing guilt which had hovered over us before.

SHARON: I'll say he was satisfied! It was a rare day when we had intercourse less than three times. We did it first thing in the morning; Cliff came home at lunch to make love again; then he wanted more in the evening. Nobody can imagine the sexual energy packed into those 125 pounds!

CLIFF: I once heard a quote, "A guy marries thinking the girl will never change; a girl marries thinking she will change the guy." There's a lot of truth to that. It seems to me that in our country, where girls try hard to attract the male admirers' attention, and the males are the aggressors, it's easy for a girl to spin a web, to hint at a marriage that looks enticing.

Maybe I was blind before our wedding, I don't know. But I was unprepared for the ways Sharon would change.

Weight was a big problem. She had worked hard before our marriage to be slim and attractive. She had always been a little chunky, but her Italian good looks made up for the excess pounds. During our engagement she tried to stay slim—a smooth complexion, dark eyes, shiny black hair made her appealing—and she kept up the fight for a little while after we were married. But gradually she started hitting the snacks and adding a few "winter pounds" until soon she became physically repulsive to me. I was ashamed of my wife.

Then her behavior changed. Before our marriage, I had made it very clear what kind of lifestyle I needed. I wanted a clean, simple place with a minimum of furniture, a minimum of clothes, and no frills. In addition I thought we ought to give away as much money as possible. Sharon knew that was a moral issue with me; I believe Christ wants us to identify with the poor. And yet after a while, she started complaining. She wanted new clothes to keep pace with other teachers around her. She wanted nicer furniture, a new bedspread, a new set of glassware.

I began to feel like a fortress besieged by invading armies. First I relented to marry sooner than I wanted, under her pressure. Now she nagged me about our lifestyle, about when we should have kids, about everything.

SHARON: There's another side to that. Cliff never gave me the support I needed. OK, I admit I made some mistakes early on. We'd go out with another couple and I would dominate the conversation with talk he considered trite. He'd always want to talk about materialism or pacifism or some abstract topic like that. I wanted advice on how to grow vegetables indoors. But he never expressed his feelings in a nice way. He'd cut me down in public, interrupt me in the middle of a sentence with a "Sharon, you don't know what you're talking about."

I like to play games—table games and card games. Cliff hates them, so naturally we didn't play.

After a year of submission and servitude, I began to see that marriage was a pretty good deal—but only for him. He worked eight hours a day, but so did I. I also did all the housework, cooked all the meals, worked hard at satisfying his unquenchable sexual appetite. And, for his sake I lost twenty pounds and gave away my excess possessions. Cliff's convictions on lifestyle became mine as well. Where was I getting support? When I tried to change things, I got accused of nagging; he claimed I had agreed to a marriage situation and now I was trying to squirm out of it. What was he doing to make me happy?

The sex thing—we've been married almost four years, and I've never had one orgasm. I have desires, even sexual fantasies. The Italian in me burns. But two and a half years of crummy sex ruined me. I learned sex while listening for footsteps, in fear of discovery. Cliff regularly felt fulfilled; I never did. I don't know what it feels like to be sexually fulfilled; I feel almost nothing now. All our sex life has been built on his convenience. Cliff has never worked at foreplay, and he's never been affectionate in public. The way he treats me says to me that I'm undesirable, that he doesn't want me.

CLIFF: Well, it's true. Sharon is undesirable to me. She's gained weight, she wears sloppy clothes, she nags me—what is there to desire? She doesn't seem like the girl I asked to marry me. I've been betrayed. She's changed on me, and I'm not willing to accept her now.

I've learned that Sharon is more manually oriented than I am. At night, when it's quiet and I want to read, she always wants to do something—go bowling or knit or putter around the kitchen. I can understand that, but why did she make such an effort to seem intellectual before we were married? Why did I have to wait to find out she was faking interest in my favorite subjects?

Sometimes I feel I love her. She's faithful to me, and tries to please me. Intellectually I can convince myself that she's a good wife. But emotionally, I'm bored. She doesn't excite me.

SHARON: It's pretty obvious, both to us and the people who know us, that we don't support each other. Whenever we try, by saying "I love you" or complimenting each other, it seems mechanical and forced, for we both know deep problems lurk underneath which have not been resolved. Cliff is by nature less dependent than I, and he can survive without support more easily. I've had to turn to others who can build me up as a person.

As a teacher I'm respected both by my students and my fellow teachers. Other teachers let me know that I'm physically appealing to them. Sometimes I feel guilty, but usually it pleases me to know that a man thinks I'm appealing. If I didn't get that feeling from other men, I might believe Cliff's low concept of me, and then I'd be saddled with self-image problems.

CLIFF: We can talk calmly, in each other's presence, about our differences now, although you can still sense an accusing tone. It was not always as calm. Formerly, whenever an argument would come we would drag out our weapons: various levels of threats and accusations which built to a threat of divorce. And then the argument would end, with no constructive solution.

Both of us were plagued with seething hatred which was sealed inside, like a boiling pot, fueling us. When we'd argue, all the pent-up steam would explode. We'd have violent arguments over issues as mundane as burnt peas. We would throw food, physically hit each other—pretty courageous for me, since she outweighs me and is stronger! It was absurd, and we'd always feel ashamed after the storm subsided. We had thought of ourselves as reserved and sophisticated, yet we acted like TV soap-opera quarrelers. Sometimes I would storm out of the bedroom and spread a sleeping bag on the floor to avoid sleeping with Sharon.

Recognizing that we needed help with our marriage, we studied together some books which might be helpful. *I'm OK— You're OK* was the most helpful because it put tags on our roles. The authors, leaders in Transactional Analysis, teach people to recognize their behavior as the behavior of a Parent, a Child, or an Adult. For example, if Sharon would pout when I didn't notice her new curtains (Child) I would take on a haughty Parent tone and say something like "Come on, are you such a baby that I have to follow you around noticing all your toys?" We worked at talking to each other like Adults. We tried to replace accusing sentences such as "You're making me angry" and "Can't you understand anything?" with "I'm getting angry" and "What don't you understand about what I said?" At least we concentrated on our communication and became civil again.

Some people would see our problems as spiritual problems. And they may be right. In my parents' terms I've "grown away from the Lord." We don't read the Bible, we seldom pray, and we haven't found a decent church. I expend most of my religious energies reacting against the fundamentalism and legalism of my background. We haven't experienced the aliveness of Christ in our lives.

My whole life pattern is to react. I react against hypocrisy, so I'm afraid to have faith. I react against Sharon's changes and feel cheated, so I have a lousy marriage. But it's not so easy to stop. We've been rolling on these same tracks for four or five years now. I don't know how to switch to a new track. I think about Christian things, but I don't really know what a personal relationship with Christ should be.

SHARON: I agree that our spiritual vacuum affects our lives. I'm not happy with my Christian life at all. I can point to some things that have caused this state, too. We moved to a small town in Idaho because we wanted a clean, simple lifestyle without a lot of materialistic pressures. But by doing so we isolated ourselves from most sources of help. We don't go to church. The farmers around here are interested in a different type of service than we want on a Sunday morning.

The biggest factor, probably, is that we're apart from any Christian fellowship. We both need models to look up to, people whose lives demonstrate that Christ is alive. We need to see Christ working in marriages to believe he can make a difference in ours.

CLIFF: Probably this description of our marriage comes across like we're on the verge of divorce. We're not. We've talked about it, and decided to stay with each other even though sometimes we're both miserable. That's a healthy sign, I think. We know we can survive even when the days are tense and strained. We've learned to give in to each other's orneriness so totally that we get beaten down. We're trying to go halfway to make the other person happy. We still play at war, sometimes; yet we know the rules, and I don't think we really damage each other.

What's sad is that we're missing out on the joy of life. We have so few joys left. Sometimes the spark returns—when we take skiing trips in the Rockies, when we visit old college friends and I feel nostalgic and affectionate. But mostly our lives are a boring routine.

Neither of us would have predicted our problems when we got married. I suppose no one does, else fewer people would marry. Somehow my Christian hope deep within me has not been stilled. I still pray that a couple who has found answers will lovingly help us find the way. Or perhaps we will find a way to turn to God and let his love and forgiveness heal the scars and bleeding wounds of our marriage. Forgiveness, that's a hard word, one we're just beginning to learn about. . . .

WHAT DO YOU THINK ABOUT THE DOMINYS?

Ironing Out the Differences

Like the Dominys, all young couples look for ways to adjust to differences they encounter. Distinguished marriage professor Richard Klemer lists three common styles.[1]

1. *Accommodation:* One partner gives in to the other and "puts up with" the difference. This may range from complete acceptance to grumbling toleration. Klemer says accommodation must be healthily balanced out—one partner cannot be giving in all the time.

2. *Alteration:* One partner agrees to change his behavior and attitudes for the sake of the other.

3. *Aggression:* Neither partner gives in and the conflict escalates.

Did you spot all three styles of adjustments in the Dominys? Which seemed to work best for them?

Which style do you use in your own marriage most often? Are you satisfied with the way you resolve differences?

Sex Matters

Sharon Dominy claims that sex conflict is at the heart of their differences. If she were more sexually appealing and met Cliff's sexual needs, she says, the other problems would work themselves out.

Most marriage counselors would disagree with Sharon. They view sex problems as a *result* of a weak relationship, not a *cause*. There are 168 hours in a week, and only a few of them are actually spent in having intercourse. The Dominys' sex problems are extreme compared to those of most couples, but the basic issues involved crop up in nearly every marriage.

Cliff's desire for frequency of sex is well above the national norm of two to four times a week, yet Sharon accepted his needs and accommodated them. Do you think she was right in doing so, even though she was not getting satisfaction?

In advice to his daughter, Charlie Shedd counseled, "It is not true, in my counseling experience, that both parties to the union need the same results every time. I have read some writers who say that a man must be able to bring his wife to a climax on every occasion of sexual love. In my judgment there is just one thing wrong with this supposition—it simply isn't so. Some women tell me that they love to minister to their husbands' emotional needs even when they care nothing at all about physical culmination for themselves." [2] (Of course, Shedd's statement applies more to normal situations with better interchange than the Dominys' experience.)

Author Richard Klemer concludes, "The initial step toward sexual adjustment in any marriage is greater understanding and acceptance of each partner's expectations and attitudes by the other partner. To do this, it is first necessary for each partner to understand that, however right or wrong his mate's feelings appear, they *are* his feelings. Ordinarily, these feelings were building up just as strongly and for just as long a period of time in one partner as in the other. Neither partner is able to change his feelings overnight. The second step that both partners must take to improve their sexual relationship is to explore each other's feelings by talking together." [3]

The Good Times

Both Cliff and Sharon reminisce nostalgically about the "good old days" of their first year of marriage. Many couples married four or five years tend to view those early days sentimentally. They laugh about the early budget problems, the crazy idiosyncracies, the times of inexpensive fun. Actually, many of their good feelings spring from their commitment back then to work together with understanding. Often the first year of marriage, a couple's commitment level to "make the marriage work" is high. As the Dominys' marriage shows, that will to succeed can fade with time.

If a couple thinks of love as a feeling, they can become embittered when it seems to dissolve over the years. If they see it as a decision-commitment, they will realize that *they* determine when love is present or not.

The Trap

Those marriages which are already intimate often move toward deeper intimacy. But those marriages which are sliding apart drift even further downward. The Dominys would agree that their marriage has drifted steadily apart. They are like two porcupines, both with quills raised, trying to settle down close to each other.

Bernard Wiese and Urban Steinmetz describe a situation like that of the Dominys as the "time of misery": "We see a picture of two people, the wife standing at one side of the room, the husband the other, both saying to each other, 'I will love you when you love me.' Neither is willing to move from this position and the marriage remains in the miserable stage. Unfortunately, this period lasts in some marriages all of the couple's lives. Neither one is able to accept responsibility for his own failures, but blames the other, and scapegoats by projecting his weaknesses on the other.

"How does the couple move from a 'time of misery' to a 'time of awakening'? Basically, the couple moves there by facing marriage as a practical, down-to-earth experience that they have to build. After spending a great deal of time trying to change their partner, they take a look at themselves and say, 'If this is going to be a better marriage, I'm going to have to work to make it better.' This is where real love essentially begins in marriage." [4]

Using this definition, has real love ever begun in the Dominys' marriage? In yours?

The Test

One couple who have written about marriage, Joseph and Lois Bird, claim they have found a good test of a good marriage.[5] Ask a couple, "Who gives the most in your marriage?" In a good marriage, each partner answers that the other gives most.

Getting Unstuck

If you find yourself stuck in a position like the Dominys', where neither partner is budging, here are two exercises which may help move the logjam:

1. *Act As-If.* Agree for one day that you will both act as if you were in love with each other. Watch your tone of voice in speaking: does it support, build up your partner? What about your facial expressions? Are you consciously going out of your way to do things for your partner? Remind yourself all day to act as if you were in love. Then, at the end of the day, discuss the experience with your partner. What made this day different? Could it happen again?

Other as-if suggestions: Act as if you respected your partner; as if you completely trusted him; as if this were the last day you would ever be together.[6]

2. *Concentrate on the good things.*

Charlie Shedd tells of one couple, Bob and Helen J, who impressed him with their love and happiness. Even after many years, they seemed radiantly in love. After a wonderful dinner at their house, he couldn't help asking their secret so he could pass it on to the many unhappy couples he knew. Bob recited this story:

"We had a terrible time when we were first married. In fact, we even talked about calling it quits. Then we read something that gave us an idea. We decided to make a list of all the things we didn't like about each other. Of course, it was hard, but Helen gave me hers and I gave her mine. It was pretty rough reading. Some of the things we had never said out loud or shared in any way.

"Next, we did something which might seem foolish, so I hope you won't laugh. We went out to the trash basket in the backyard and burned those two lists of bad things. We watched them go up in smoke and put our arms around each other for the first time in a long while.

"Then we went back into the house and made a list of all the good things we could dig up about each other. This took some time, since we were pretty down on our marriage. But we kept at it and when we finished we did another thing which might look silly. Come on back to the bedroom and I'll show you."

Bob took Charlie Shedd to the bedroom, where the two lists were mounted in two plain maple frames. In one was the list of good things Helen could see in Bob. In the other was his scribbled list of her virtues.

"If we have any secret," Bob continued, "I guess this is it. We agreed to read these things at least once a day. Of course, we know them by heart now. I couldn't begin to tell you what they've done for me. I recite them to myself sometimes when I'm driving the car or waiting for a customer. When I hear fellows complain about their wives, I think of my list and thank my lucky stars. Funny, too, the more I consider the good she sees in me, the more I try to be like that. And when I really understood her good points, I tried all the harder to build on them. Now I think she's the most wonderful person in the world. I guess she sort of likes me too. That's all there is to it!"[7]

Good marriages don't happen spontaneously. They're work.

Marriage has enough conflicts already. Sex should be the one time when the couple takes time out for a celebration.

CHAPTER SIX

Deciphering

GRANT AND KATHY CHILTON

Grant and Kathy met in an ideally romantic setting. Both were working at a summer camp nestled among the Colorado Rockies. Teenage campers were segregated by sex and Grant supervised the boys, who were situated on a long stretch of beach along a pristine mountain lake. Kathy stayed with the girls on a nine-acre island, so all their dates began when Grant roared across the lake in a Chris-Craft. Around them, jutting abruptly from the lake, were towering snowcaps. For dates, the two would glide into a secluded cove and talk under the empty mountain sky.

Grant first expressed love for Kathy after that summer, while he was traveling alone for several months in France. ("It's risky enough to tell a girl you love her without being sure of her response. You should try it when you have to wait two weeks for her reply!")

Early in their marriage, the Chiltons clashed over a problem which plagues many partners: unexpected moods and an inability to communicate.

KATHY: We came to know each other quickly in the camp, where it was easy to find solitude. Even on my nine-acre island, secluded spots were always within a short walk. Pine trees crowded close to the cabins and huge boulders blocked off areas ideal for long, private talks.

Grant's family was very verbal. Visiting them later, I was surprised by the rounds of good-natured arguments which echoed around the dinner table. No one backed off from an argument, and even the younger kids seemed free to share deep feelings.

My family had been just the opposite—reserved and tight-lipped. I can remember long silences at our dinner table. Even when Father was consumed by tensions from his job, he never talked about it. We sensed he had had a bad day when he would grip the arms of his chair until his knuckles turned white. Mother became tense and quiet when Father was troubled, but neither of them talked.

When I was in the ninth grade, Mother died of cancer, and then I had no one to confide in. I remember wrapping my arms around our Saint Bernard, pouring out my sorrow and loneliness to him.

Grant showered me with attention. He loved to orchestrate elaborate schemes to surprise me with a present. For our engagement, he took me on a boat ride to Elk Cove. While we were sitting there, a camp employee approached in a sputtering motorboat and handed Grant an envelope, telling him, "Grant, I'm sorry to interrupt you at a time like this, but there's an emergency. You'll have to go back to the camp. Read this and you'll understand."

The emergency message in the envelope? It was a poem Grant had composed to propose to me. And that hard lump I had felt in his pocket was a diamond ring!

GRANT: We were together every day from our engagement on through our marriage the next summer. Each of us learned to probe, to find out what areas were touchy and sensitive.

The biggest tension point between us, even in engagement, stemmed from Kathy's reserved, noncommunicative upbringing. She was not used to talking about feelings.

Sometimes, quick and sudden as a mountain thunderstorm, Kathy would cloud up and climb behind a depressed, silent mask. I would plead with her to talk, but she'd insist, "Nothing's wrong." I knew better, and I was determined to break through and uncover what she was hiding from me. Those mysterious moods would drag on for two or three days.

One incident forced us both to confront the depression cycle. We were living in Denver at the time, and one Sunday we decided to visit my brother in Colorado Springs, fifty miles south. Though it was cool, we had an afternoon picnic beside a trout stream. My brother's van was equipped with four stereo speakers, and while hamburgers were cooking, we opened all the van doors and turned up our favorite music. It was delightful: the crisp fall scene of yellow aspens, the music echoing through the canyons, the smell of charcoal-broil. Just after the picnic, while we were chasing my brother's kids and rock-hopping in the creek, one of these moods hit Kathy.

I couldn't understand it. Nothing had happened to cause tension between us. How could anything negative spoil such a postcard-perfect scene? Kathy sat alone in the van while we continued our fun. The temperature began dropping by three in the afternoon, and we packed up and headed toward my brother's house. He lived twenty minutes away, and even before we arrived, the first snow flurries of fall had begun.

We had planned to stay through dinner and then drive back. But by mealtime two inches of snow already covered the ground. Evening weather reports warned motorists to stay off the roads to Denver. The storm had hit there first, and snowplows were still mothballed from the summer, so road-clearing was sluggish. I had a sensible idea: "Honey, why don't we just spend the night here. We'll avoid the hassle of driving through snow, and tomorrow morning we can get up an hour early and still make it to work on time." She shook her head no.

I persisted. "Honey, are you sure?" She shot me a glare of irritation and said aloud, "Grant, I think we should leave tonight." I pressed for an explanation, but she wouldn't give one. She'd only say, "No, I want to go home."

Naturally, my brother and his wife detected the ripples of tension, and all other conversation ceased. Finally, I excused ourselves to the hall and asked, "Kathy, are you absolutely refusing to stay here tonight?" She lowered her head and nodded yes.

"Then, let's go," I said angrily, heading for my coat. Five minutes later we were in our car pointed toward Denver, fighting traffic and slush.

KATHY: I knew Grant was angry with me. My sudden mood that afternoon baffled me too, but I did not want to spend the night with his brother's family.

We drove the first ten minutes in silence. From experience I knew Grant's mind was spinning, constructing a case against me. It would begin as one of his lectures and probably end with me in tears. I couldn't understand. We hadn't planned to spend the night—why was that so important to him?

He began, "Kathy, we're going home tonight, as you insisted. But this is the last time a scene like this will occur between us. I *will not be* manipulated by your negative feelings. From now on, if you want to alter a decision, you'll have to articulate your reasons to me. I won't allow you to play these emotional games."

He told me about his father, who was very forceful and eloquent. Grant's mother could rarely win an argument from him; he was always more articulate and persuasive. Instead, she countered by remaining silent and discouraged. Since Grant's father was also a sensitive and compassionate man, that would shake him up. He found it difficult to handle her unexpressed, negative feelings. As a result, he frequently abandoned the issue at hand and worked toward reconciliation, "peace at any price." The issue was often lost and left unresolved. It appeared to Grant that his father had really been manipulated by the lack of communication. He had watched that cycle run through their marriage for too many years, he said, and he wouldn't allow it to seep into ours.

While Grant lectured, I remained silent, staring at the snowflakes on my window. What could I say? I didn't know why I was in a bad mood, but that didn't change the situation. Grant was making me feel guilty, but I honestly had no idea what to tell him when he demanded an explanation.

The emotional tension and the strain of driving in a snowstorm combined to make Grant as angry as I'd seen him. Cars were sliding into ditches on both sides of the road. We had slowed to about twenty miles an hour, and whenever we had to stop suddenly, our car fishtailed to the right. Grant maneuvered behind a tractor trailer to follow his tracks, but the truck's huge tires kicked up a constant stream of wet snow onto our windshield.

Grant continued lecturing, and soon I began crying. It was a miserable scene.

GRANT: I wasn't mad at Kathy for being in a bad mood, or for insisting on driving home that night—even though it was an unwise decision because of the weather; I was mad because she wouldn't tell me what was bothering her. I wanted to help, to solve the issue, but I couldn't begin without knowing what the issue was. I talked, Kathy cried, the roads got more dangerous. . . .

Finally, just five miles from Denver I pulled off the road into a rest area and turned to her. "Kathy, I'm not going further until we find out what is bugging you." She insisted she couldn't help me.

"OK, Kathy, I'm going to start making a list. You tell me when you think I hit on why you were upset. Was it a physical reason? Were you sexually uptight?" She shook her head no.

"Was it a spiritual reason?"

"No."

"Did I do something at the picnic to upset you?"

"No."

I continued, listing every reason I could think of. She had stopped crying now, and was concentrating on my questions, trying for an answer. Finally, out of the blue, I hit one that evoked a response. "Did my brother's children bother you?" She started to shake her head again, then paused. As she looked up I could see the first flash of insight in her eyes.

"Yes, they did bother me. They're spoiled, and I hate whiny, demanding kids. After spending all day with them, I just didn't want to face them all evening too."

Kathy's expression showed that the thought was as much a revelation to her as it was to me. The tension broke. I reached out for her and said, "Honey, that's OK. If you had told me, I would have understood. I would have gladly driven back tonight without that fight. But I have to know what you're thinking. I can't read your mind."

KATHY: I had repressed my feelings for so long that I was out of touch with them. I had no idea why I had jumped into a bad mood. As soon as Grant forced me to dig up the reason I felt relieved. The depression snapped at once. Grant was happy, I was happy. We held each other, drove back onto the road, and continued home.

Some time later it happened again. When Grant asked for Swedish pancakes for breakfast on Saturday, I looked through the recipe card file I'd inherited from my mother until I found her favorite recipe. Swedish pancakes had been a Saturday morning tradition in our family, and I felt confident as I mixed the ingredients.

I called Grant from the living room, and he came in, grinning, saying, "I can't wait. I've been looking forward to these pancakes since the day we were married." He arranged the toppings —blueberries, raspberries, whipped cream, apricot preserves— on the table and sat down. When I brought him the steaming pancakes, I expected to see a smile of anticipation.

Instead he looked disappointed. My heart sank.

"What's wrong?" I asked. "Didn't you want Swedish pancakes for breakfast?"

"Well . . . yes," he said. "These look fine. But I thought Swedish pancakes are supposed to be thin and light. These are thick, and sort of lumpy-looking."

Immediately one of my depressions hit. We mechanically ate breakfast, the only sounds being the clink of silverware. But inside I was just as devastated as I'd been the day at his brother's. Grant knew it instantly, and after breakfast, he asked to talk.

Once again, Grant asked if we could go over a check list of things that could have upset me. I agreed, and he started the round of questions. "Did I offend your cooking in general? Are you upset because I didn't help in the kitchen?"

Finally he hit one that made sense. As he probed, I realized that I felt Grant had rejected my mother by rejecting her favorite recipe. I had always been defensive and protective about my mother, trying to keep anything from encroaching on her memories. And when Grant lightly criticized my pancakes, it triggered a bell in me which said, "He's cutting down your mother." It was silly, of course; my mother had died before I'd even met Grant, and he wasn't cutting her down. But it was just as real to me as if he had criticized her.

Again, as soon as the reaction was explained, I felt relief and acceptance. Grant hugged me, and he was satisfied with the explanation.

GRANT: This pattern was repeated often in the early days of our marriage. Kathy's moods came to her untagged, seemingly without reason. I had to help her discover what was really bothering

her. At first it took as long as two days before she'd be willing
to talk. I really believe it wasn't because she was withholding
something from me; she didn't know what was wrong. It was a
thrill to see the time span between onset of mood and solution
dip down from two days to one day, to four hours, to ten
minutes.

Every time she'd hit a bad mood, we'd talk. If I supported her,
and assured her I was trying to help, she opened up and eventually together we'd come up with an explanation. As soon as I
knew the reason, I understood her reactions, and she did too.
She almost began to look forward to those talks when we would
uncover what was wrong.

We've been married four years, and Kathy now can almost
always tag the emotion and find an explanation herself, within
minutes. That doesn't mean all negative emotions are cast out
so quickly; sometimes we both need times of distance, when we
work through something on our own. But Kathy feels much more
in control of herself.

There's a principle in psychology that a person who has repressed emotions and sensations for a long time often can't learn
to know himself without opening up to another person. He needs
dialogue—someone who cares enough to lovingly listen to him
and help him get perspective. It was beautiful to be a part of
Kathy's process of working through hangups. I think it is an
example of marriage at its best.

KATHY: My desire to please other people had made me afraid
to assert myself and let my true feelings emerge. Soon I learned
that Grant wanted me to share my feelings. When I bottled them
inside, inevitably they leaked out in some conflict.

I learned to truly participate in decisions. Previously, if Grant
asked, "Honey, I've got a day off tomorrow; what would you
like to do?" I'd ask him for some options. He'd say, "Well, we
could drive to Vail and ski, or we could go to a museum in
Denver, or find a concert, or see a movie—you name it." I would
think, *Let's see, Grant loves to ski, therefore I'll say skiing.*

Grant's eyes would light up when I answered and he'd be
fastening the ski rack to our car in five minutes. But I hadn't
been honest. The next day, while Grant was slaloming down the
trails, I'd sit in the lodge feeling like a jilted old maid. Skiing

wasn't something we could enjoy together, because we skied on different levels. Grant was bored with the beginner's slopes; I was afraid of the advanced slopes.

After a series of conflicts, I began to see that Grant wasn't asking me my opinion as a trap to get his own way. He legitimately wanted to make me happy. He was submitting to my desires, but I was thwarting him.

We still go skiing, and sometimes it's at my request because I know how happy it makes Grant. But often I come up with a crazy idea he's never thought of.

GRANT: While Kathy had to learn to get in touch with her feelings and communicate verbally in marriage, I had to learn the intricacies of communicating physically. I suppose every couple goes through the nervous process of finding sexual compatibility. The unusual thing about our sex relationship is that on the honeymoon everything worked perfectly. We both were satisfied, without hangups or fears. In fact, on the third night we reached a simultaneous climax, something which is usually not achieved without a lot of practice.

But that was a fluke, it seemed. Because as soon as we were home, getting adjusted as newlyweds, our sex life skidded. I always reached a climax, usually quite early in intercourse, but Kathy did not. She often did not feel pleasure in intercourse. Many times I would end up physically satisfied, while Kathy would be in tears. She felt like a failure as a wife and lover, because sex had not been a shared experience.

I tried not to pressure Kathy, but she continued feeling guilty and a failure. I was unskilled at knowing just what a woman wanted, I must admit, and Kathy could not express it to me well.

KATHY: One problem haunting me was a bad experience I had had with another girl. When I went to college, I was very lonely. I was a thousand miles from home, and I sought solace in the close friendship of another girl. We had some sex experiences together which started innocently, but led into something which bored a painful sense of guilt into me. It was very hard for me to bring up the subject with Grant, but the experiences were affecting our love life. Whenever he tried manual stimulation, the guilt would flash back and I would recoil from him.

I'm not sure how I got the nerve to approach the subject, but doing so brought us an amazing discovery: talking about sex can be as stimulating and exciting as physical caressing. Those moments when we opened up were precious, intimate secrets that only the two of us would ever be in on. It developed a bond of closeness between us.

When I told Grant about the past experience, he was very warm and understanding. He shared with me some of his own struggles with masturbation that he had never told anyone. We both exposed secrets, and it pulled us together.

I knew I needed help to tackle the problem of my hangups, and to deal with our ignorance about sex, so I asked my gynecologist, who is incredibly understanding and trustworthy, to talk with Grant and me together.

I imagine everything the doctor told us was in marriage manuals, but it helped me to hear the facts from an understanding person. He convinced me that manual stimulation is not dirty or distasteful. And he gave us some helpful hints. He told Grant it would help if he worked on bringing me to a climax first. He also explained that to a woman sex is a much more wholistic, thorough act. Dressing up and eating out may be an integral part of preparing a woman for sex. And I have much more desire for intimate foreplay than Grant does.

Grant and I took the advice well. By getting the problem in the open, we overcame our nervousness about it, and we went home with a sense of adventure, both working together to have a mutually pleasing sex life.

No wife would hesitate to give her husband explicit instructions about scratching a hard-to-reach itch: "No, to the right, down a little, harder . . . ah, harder; oh, that feels good." But somehow we have a hard time giving our husbands directions on sex techniques. It's almost as if we expect them automatically to know what pleases us. Of course, that's impossible. How could Grant know if I didn't tell him?

GRANT: In small groups I've talked to many young couples with sex problems. Often their sex life is tense and full of conflict. It's something that they have to "get over." It's a blockage between them, not a coming together.

Marriage has enough conflicts already. Sex should be the one time when the couple takes time out for a celebration. The only way that happened with us both was for us both to be honest, admit the awkwardness and seek help.

A sexual life should keep growing, and we've tried to keep adding new dimensions to ours. Just recently we started reading a book called *Ideal Marriage: Its Physiology and Technique* by a Dutch physician. We leave it in the car and whenever we go on trips together, whoever is not driving reads it aloud. It has helped us immensely to get the issues into the daylight and to talk about them.

In both these issues we've worked through—communicating verbally and communicating physically—the key has been to see the problem as *our* problem, one we share. If I had looked on Kathy's bad moods as her problem and taken the attitude, "Well, you've got to find your own way of working that out, but I demand you improve," the result would have been tragic.

And the sex thing: she could have refused to talk and gone frigid, or said, "Well, I'm not going to help you because I don't feel comfortable talking about it. You're the one with the strong sex drives. Find your own solution." Those sealed-off areas, where the couples split apart, each going his own direction, are the danger signs that a relationship is in trouble.

God has given us a goal to understand each other and help each other. We must reckon with anything which interrupts that goal. We genuinely want to help each other. Marriage is not a possession one of us has; it's a *mutual* possession. When one of us hurts, we both hurt. When one of us grows, we both grow.

WHAT DO YOU THINK ABOUT THE CHILTONS?

Hiding Something

Often a sexual experience like Kathy had festers inside a person who is afraid to share it with a partner. Are you keeping deep secrets from your partner because of guilt or shame or fear? There is no need to dredge up the past for the mere sake of exposing it, but often a marriage partner can help you deal with a bad experience by proving to you that you are accepted despite it.

The Clinebells' classic book on intimacy records that intimacy grows as couples dare to risk greater openness.[1] We can tend to hide our weaknesses, afraid of spoiling our strong image with our partner. When one partner leads from weakness, admitting his faults, however, it can be an important bridge to intimacy.

Robert Bower, professor at Fuller Seminary, gives this guiding principle, "When a spouse asks a question, it is probable that he possesses sufficient ego strength and has mobilized enough emotional resources to withstand the emotional impact of any answer whatever. The person who cannot handle the impact of an answer to such a question because it would be shattering to his personality will usually repress and refuse to ask it." [2]

Celebrate Sex

Grant and Kathy speak of sex as celebration. Too often in marriage sex causes tension and misunderstanding. What do you think makes the difference with the Chiltons?

Sex is most meaningful when it unites body, mind, and heart. When sex is separated into a bodily function, it can be harmful. (Consider the effect of a rape on a woman: it can crush her emotionally because her physical secrets are seized from her without the cooperation of mind and heart.)

Sexual intercourse is like a language, a way of communicating that cannot be matched in words, music, or any other way. It is a language of love shared by only two partners. Charlie Shedd calls sex "a God-ordained means of assuring your partner that he is the most important person in the world right here, right now." [3]

Is sex a celebration for you or a tension-producer? Have you talked it over with your partner? Would you feel free to seek professional help as Kathy did? Ask yourself, "What does sex add to our relationship? Would our relationship be essentially different without it?"

How Do You Rate?

By overcoming barriers to verbal communication and physical communication, Grant and Kathy opened the way toward greater intimacy. Often a person who needs more intimacy in one area fails to inform his partner. As a good discussion-starter, consider this intimacy checkup by Harold and Charlotte Clinebell: [4]

MARITAL INTIMACY CHECKUP*
(Instructions: After discussing each area, check the blanks that apply to your relationship.)

Facts of Intimacy	Both Desire Improve- ment	Wife Desires Improve- ment	Husband Desires Improve- ment	Both Satisfied
1. Sexual Intimacy				
2. Emotional Intimacy (Being tuned to each other's wavelength)				
3. Intellectual Intimacy (Closeness in the world of ideas)				
4. Aesthetic Intimacy (Sharing in acts of creating beauty)				
5. Creative Intimacy (Sharing in acts of creating together)				
6. Recreational Intimacy (Relating in exper- iences of fun and play)				
7. Work Intimacy (Closeness of sharing common tasks)				
8. Crisis Intimacy (Closeness in coping with problems and pain)				
9. Conflict Intimacy (Facing and struggling with differences)				

*"Marital Intimacy Checkup Chart" (pp. 37–38) in THE INTIMATE MARRIAGE by Howard J. Clinebell, Jr., and Charlotte H. Clinebell. Copyright © 1970 by Howard J. Clinebell, Jr., and Charlotte H. Cline- bell. By permission of Harper & Row, Publishers, Inc.

Facts of Intimacy	Both Desire Improve-ment	Wife Desires Improve-ment	Husband Desires Improve-ment	Both Satisfied
10. Commitment Intimacy (Mutuality derived from common self-investment)				
11. Spiritual Intimacy (The we-ness in sharing ultimate concerns)				
12. Communication Intimacy (The source of all types of true intimacy)				
Total				

In those areas in which both of you desire improvement, discuss specific next steps which you feel can be taken to increase the degree of mutuality and meaningful closeness in each area. If you agree on specific action in one or more areas, decide on how you will go about implementing your plan. If you agree on what you want to do in several areas, decide on which should have priority. Jot down the main ideas for action. If you cannot agree on any concrete plan in any area in which you both desire change, you may need to consult a marriage counselor.

We read books on marriage which say the key is the self-sacrificing giving of each partner. But in our relationship, that's dangerous. It's as if there's a giant power struggle going on and we've both only got so much ammunition.

CHAPTER SEVEN

A Question of Power

BRAD AND MARIA STEFFAN

Those of us who watched Brad and Maria fall in love knew their future could be explosive. Both were intense, dominant persons. Put them in a party situation and soon the action and conversation would revolve around them. They were attracted to each other's strength, but that mutual strength set them up for a marriage rife with conflict. Neither personality had a noticeable streak of submission.

Brad had grown up with a father and two brothers (his mother died while delivering him). Taught that aggression and dominance were the important male traits, he carved out a very rational, self-sufficient life. No one saw Brad in an emotional outburst; he was controlled under all circumstances.

Maria was raised in a family with three brothers. She did not enjoy housework and cooking chores, but preferred carpentry or repairing lawnmowers. And in high school, Maria always dreamed about a career, never about marriage.

Love surprised both Brad and Maria so suddenly and powerfully that their personalities seemed to flipflop. Brad became gentle and understanding, searching for ways to please Maria. Maria was coy and sexy, looking to Brad as the leader. Their friends were amazed at the changes forged by love.

Marriage, though, brought out a curious blend of the new personalities and the old. Brad's stubbornness emerged, clashing with Maria's fiery independence. After three years of marriage, if friends asked Brad if he was glad he had married, he would reply, "I can't really say that I am. It's much different than I expected—much different."

MARIA: Brad liked to say negative things about our marriage back then, and they usually got back to me. It was one of his techniques of inspiring guilt in me. He uprooted me from home, moved me fifteen hundred miles to take a job he liked, forced me to learn to cook in a tiny sweatbox of a kitchen, and then expected me to come out in silk lingerie and play his mistress for the evening. I refused. Doing the cooking and the traditional "wifely" roles were concessions enough. After all, I worked an eight-hour day also.

What did I get out of marriage? Once in a while he'd take me out to dinner or to a movie. He did not give me recognition as a wife. He rarely commented on my cooking or on the little ways I tried to please him. It didn't impress him that I had sacrificed by leaving a good job opportunity to follow him across the country.

After a year or two, we both felt burned by marriage.

BRAD: Resentments and misunderstandings soon accumulated into a massive mountain separating us. Not being raised around girls, I had little appreciation for the differences between guys and girls in our society. In our family, we discussed decisions, arrived at a consensus and acted. If one of us had a gripe, it was stated clearly and directly. We could handle honesty and directness.

Though I was unaware of it at the time, I can see now that I mistakenly expected the same direct approach from Maria. I assumed that when she said something she meant it. But Maria was different; she spoke in code sentences, her words cloaking innuendos and hidden meanings. I should have picked up some clues while we were dating in high school. Whenever she faced a big event like a speech, she'd grouse and complain about it weeks beforehand. "I'll do terrible," she'd say. "Whenever I have to speak, I freeze, my voice shakes, and I get a mental block."

I'd argue with her, trying to build her confidence, but she'd rebuff all my attempts to help her. Then, after the big event, she'd saunter out of speech class whistling, her face glowing, receiving compliments from classmates.

"How'd you do?" I'd ask.

"Oh, fine," she'd say nonchalantly. "I knew I would."

I thought she was crazy. For two weeks she had made us both miserable, and now she said she'd been confident all along.

After we were married, I encountered the same trend. Whenever Maria really griped about something, I took her seriously. She'd cut down her mother and attack her sisters for being irresponsible. I would agree, supporting her argument; then she would turn and attack me!

She would come home complaining about her boorish, insensitive boss. I would agree and recommend she start looking somewhere else; then she'd get mad at me. *Do women always say the opposite of what they mean?* I wondered. Each time that happened, it would set off fireworks.

After a serious incident our third year of marriage, an idea of what was happening finally sank into my thick head. We were spending a weekend with another couple on a lake in Tennessee. Even before the trip we had been feuding and arguing, and when we reached the lake the bickering escalated to open warfare. We tossed and turned in the same bed that night, but neither of us slept. Early the next morning, I poked Maria and asked her if she wanted to go out in the rowboat with the rest of us, and she gave me no response. I was just as happy to go without her, so I quickly dressed and went for the boat ride in the morning fog.

I laughed and joked with our friends, felt the stimulating wash of the cool fog, and returned to shore refreshed and determined to patch up our argument.

As I ran ahead of the others to the screen porch, I could see Maria sitting in a white wicker chair, waiting. I opened the door, walked up to her, and before I could say a word, she announced, "Brad Steffan, I hate you. I have ever since I married you."

I stopped. All the reconciliation and forgiveness I had felt in the boat drained out of me. My mouth tightened and I stalked out of the room.

MARIA: Of course I didn't mean that I hated him. But Brad insisted on taking everything I said at face value. He wasn't sensitive to the nuances of communication. I said I hated him because I was angry. It was a way of letting off steam, and I wanted some kind of reaction out of him.

Brad wouldn't accept that. He dropped whatever issue we were fighting about and latched onto this one statement. After two horrendous days, we finally made up. How? Of course *I* had to writhe and apologize and promise I'd never say anything like that again. Brad never dealt with the real issue. He'd deal with some side-effect where I had clearly been irrational or had exaggerated.

What did I want from Brad? I wanted his love and attention and support. When I complained about a speech or my job, or a burned dinner, I wanted Brad to talk me out of it, to soothe and support me. It was my way of working out of nervousness and fear. He couldn't sense that. He'd take my words literally, then condemn me for having such an unreasonable attitude.

I wanted Brad to love me in spite of my weaknesses. He refused, insisting I deal with my weaknesses *before* he would love me. His love and acceptance were like a reward for being "a good girl" and staying cheerful and pleasant and affectionate.

Knowing the little outward display of love in his family, I can understand why Brad is like that. His father never knew how to express affection. He would reward his sons for achievement, and he ran the family like a B. F. Skinner rat-box: do good, get reward; do bad, get shocked. Brad tried the same method on me, and I wouldn't cooperate.

It just so happens that I was reared in a family that never articulated praise. I have a hungry need for praise and recognition, but Brad doesn't see that. He's too hung up on "straightening me out."

BRAD: Maria accuses me of misreading her communication. She claims the real communication is not in the words, but in the tone of voice, the gestures, the meaning behind the words. I don't like the system. I'd prefer it if everyone would be direct and honest, but I have learned to read some of her inner meanings.

There's an area of my life where I need her help—the area of sex. I feel least capable there, and I approach her hesitantly and shyly. I need a wife who can be understanding and see past my awkwardness and clumsiness.

Because Mom was dead, I never saw physical affection around our house. And until Maria, I had always been scared of girls. I felt strange and uncomfortable around them. Maria sensed it before our marriage and was very affectionate. She'd promise that when we'd get married she would lay traps for me: I would come home and find her nude in bed, waiting for me, she'd say. I liked her aggressiveness, the ease with which she talked about sex.

But after five years of marriage, I haven't been seduced yet. The only sex trap we've gotten into is how many advances of mine Maria will ignore. She'll be sitting on the couch flipping through a magazine, and I'll sit beside her and put my arm around her. I'll stroke her, give her a neck rub, play with her hair, and get no response at all. It's very hard for me to make advances toward her, and it rips me up when she acts disinterested and ignores me. Sometimes she'll suddenly get up and walk away to do something in the kitchen. We show very little physical affection to each other. Usually when I'm touching her, it means something. But she ignores me.

MARIA: How am I supposed to know when he wants sex? Whenever I misread a cue, he goes into this long sexual-anger war that can last for one or two weeks. He refuses to touch me, he's glum and often silent, and the expression on his face tells me that somewhere I missed one of his cues and I'm being punished. But I certainly cannot go to him then. I'm the one being rejected. It's up to him to make a move toward me.

BRAD: If she only knew how I burned inside. It's a risk—a gut-wrenching, fearful risk when I make a move toward her. I'm exposing myself. I'm shouting, "I have a need!" and still she ignores me. It's hard for me to admit needs—Maria gets on me for being too self-sufficient. But in sex I do admit deep, crying needs. And she doesn't detect them.

MARIA: Yes, but usually those needs don't come tagged with an "I want intercourse" signs on them. They're barely discernible gestures—a brush of his arm, a slight fondling. How am I supposed to know what he wants?

I do not have strong sexual needs. I can easily go for a month without sex and I rarely ever have an impulse to initiate sex. How can I solve his problem? He has the hangup, not me.

Before marriage, I had a few sexual experiences that scared me off. Once, I was standing on a doorstep with my boyfriend (not Brad) when I had a sudden desire for him to hold my breast. I reached down, took his hand and placed it on my breast. He went animal. He pawed me, grabbed me, practically started attacking me. It was all I could do to push him away and get inside the door.

I perform well as a sexual partner for Brad. I am not frigid; I have orgasms regularly. But if he has the high sexual energy needs, I think he should be the one to take the initiative.

There's one factor Brad hasn't mentioned. Whenever he goes into one of those sexual-anger moods, there's always a reckoning day. He'll storm and fume for a week or two. I'll wait until he's ready to talk; then he'll dump everything on me. Once he was so angry he yelled, "Maria, you've got two problems; you're *sexless* and *religionless*." He really believed that.

What does it do to me, to be beaten down and called inadequate month after month? It certainly doesn't make me *want* to become a ravishing, delicious sexual partner.

Sometimes I abhor sex. I think it's the worst part of marriage because it brings me such emotional pain. Brad has done that to me with his constant harping and haranguing. I never felt like that before marriage.

BRAD: We've talked about getting professional advice about sex, and maybe we should. I could see that I was destroying Maria. I made demands on her she couldn't fulfill. Her self-concept was withering away. So finally, after five years I came up with a sexual compromise. It's just a temporary measure, and it's not ideal. But it does solve some of our problems. I agreed to two rules: (1) Whenever I want sex, I have to ask for it verbally, so she will not misread my cues. (2) I will never expect her to make an advance. If she does, naturally it will delight me, but by agreeing to this rule, I remove all reason for blaming her for sexual failure.

But those rules remove spontaneity from our sex life. They also put Maria under subtle pressure always to say yes if I ask her, because she's scared of the consequences if she turns me down. But at least we've talked about it and reached an agreement. Hopefully, it will work toward removing the aura of fear and guilt which I've pressed down around Maria. Maybe some day we will grow to the place where our sex life is based on mutuality. Neither of us is ready for that yet.

MARIA: One problem I have had in resolving conflicts with Brad occurs because, to Brad, the only most important thing in life is to be proved right. In our arguments, he never backs down and admits he is wrong. The facts can be on my side, but somehow he will twist and rationalize so that he comes out looking like a winner. It used to infuriate me that he would make me cry. I'd hold up for a half-hour of solid argument, but then I'd collapse in tears. I could never make Brad cry. He would not back down. That history has built up in me a fear of confronting him. If I have a gripe against Brad, I never bring it to him directly, because I think the result will probably be in his favor anyway. I stifle those criticisms.

BRAD: But those criticisms don't disappear; they come out in more harmful ways. Maria chooses to release her depth charges when we're in public. She says she feels safe there, where I can't attack her. I go blind with anger when she chooses the public to stab me. It can be a minor issue, like my not helping her with cooking, or it can be a major issue, like my sexual inadequacy. But sometimes Maria will hit a weak spot with a skillfully contrived, sarcastic dig. I'm sure the couple or group we're with do not sense the iceberg of tension underneath the surface. To me, it's the most unfair thing Maria could do. Until now, I have been too insecure to open up and admit weaknesses; no one in my family ever did. I know a Christian should be vulnerable, but it takes work and a feeling of security. Having my weaknesses exposed in public is not the way for me to find that openness.

MARIA: A few times Brad has voluntarily come to me and exposed a weakness. Once he lied to me. He paints as a hobby, and he always wants to spend our extra money on new art techniques. He buys sketchboards, dyes, acrylic paints, and so on. I bug him about the expense, and he's sensitive about it.

One day he left work early and went to an art store to pick up a new brush. When I saw him that night I asked, "Did you buy anything else?" He answered no.

A few days later the truth came out. Brad came to me and said, "Maria, I hate myself for doing this, and I don't know why I did it. You caught me off guard with that question. I didn't want to start an argument between us, so I lied. I spent $40 buying new art equipment. I would have told you, but when you asked me like that, I suddenly panicked."

Brad was nervous and boylike when he told me. After all the years of being right, he was finally admitting to being wrong, and it was beautiful. It was easy for me to reach out and love him and tell him that I forgave him. I want to see the openness in our marriage where we're free to relate to each other like that. But Brad is so hesitant to show me weakness. And after being proved wrong so many times, I'm also gun-shy of showing him any weakness.

BRAD: Intellectually, I understand her complaint. But my whole background has been to fight for recognition and be proved right. My father instilled those values in me. I did not have the softening, human influence of an understanding mother. And I'm sure that fear of weakness spills over into the sexual area. It's the one realm in our marriage where Maria reigns. She can control the emotional tone of our marriage with her responses. I see her as a condescending queen, doling out sexual favors to a sputtering child.

MARIA: Brad has such a power advantage over me because he was reared in the midst of conflict. At my house, if I threw a temper tantrum, I'd run to my room and slam the door. The rest of the family went on as normal, knowing eventually I'd come around. They accepted aberrant behavior. Brad's family ground to a halt if one of the boys was upset. Immediately the others pounced on him, demanding explanations, fighting over the issue. At the supper table they acted like a pack of wolves. He learned to survive by conflict, and he expects me to carry on likewise. I can't do it.

BRAD: I still don't believe conflict is all bad. Most psychologists will tell you it's best to let your frustrations rise to the surface and bounce off someone. In fact, once I read a quote from the Roman playwright Terentius: "Great love was never lost by small quarrels. Love after the quarrel was greater than before." I think our problem is that we haven't found an acceptable common ground to fight on.

MARIA: It's very hard to imagine creative conflict when I've been the loser for so long. It's as if I've built a protective shell around myself I can't let Brad enter. I have always been competitive. I can't stand the image of the submissive, boot-licking wife. I despise the seductive, Baby Doll image of wives taught in books like *Total Woman.* I want my independence, yet I want to lean on Brad. Marriage is so confusing. I want to protect myself. I'm afraid of giving in.

We read books on marriage which say the key is the self-sacrificing giving of each partner. But in our relationship, that's dangerous. It's as if there's a giant power struggle going on and we've both only got so much ammunition. If I take the peace initiative and let Brad through my defenses, he might hurt me.

BRAD: Yes, that's true. It is a power struggle and we're both protecting our independence. But that's changing because we have gradually found our identities. However, we've found them through success at our jobs, not through mutually supporting each other. We are more complete people now, but we haven't found a way to grow together in intimacy.

We're aware of what areas are dangerous and conflict-producing, but we've just fenced off those areas. There are too many "restricted" signs in our marriage. We live out separate. lives with a few areas of overlap.

When I was dating Maria, my friends would often comment about how feisty she was. I would smile and give them this analogy: "Well, you know there are two ways to get a good horse. One is to raise him tame from a colt until he's obedient and responsive to your wishes. Another way is to find a beautiful wild stallion and break it. If you can successfully train the stallion, you'll end up with a better horse." But after being married, I realized how selfish and sexist that analogy was. Maria is not a horse to order around. She's a delicate, complex person. How can we both live as free, caring persons without crowding each other? What must we "give up" in marriage?

We had to pull apart to build trust and to stop destroying each other. We needed that time of distance. But we can't stay there. We must move on and find new areas of exploring together. We're both committed to do that.

MARIA: David Hubbard, president of Fuller Seminary, has written about power struggles such as our marriage. Power, he says, is a gift we're entrusted with. We can use it for good or for ill; that's up to us. But he claims the true test for one who handles power well is to ask, "Are you willing to give it away?" An effective businessman gives his subordinates as much power as they can handle. He's not threatened. And an effective marriage partner relinquishes power to the other partner.

In contrast, Brad and I hold onto power; we need it for the next conflict. Trust is the essential factor. Perhaps someday we can count on our trust so much that we can give away our power to each other, instead of clinging to it as a necessary defense.

WHAT DO YOU THINK ABOUT THE STEFFANS?

Out of Bounds

What did you think of the Steffans' style of arguing? Did you detect any signs of "foul play"—that is, ways of arguing that should be ruled out of bounds? Consider this list of foul play in arguments.

1. Never criticize in public.
2. Don't criticize something which can't be changed.
3. Don't store up complaints and unload them all at once.
4. Never use physical violence.
5. Don't avoid the issue by attacking *the person* or by defending yourself with a "you do the same thing" argument.
6. Don't fight to decide a winner and loser; the goal must be mutual satisfaction.
7. Don't bring up "buried hatchets"—old arguments that should have been resolved long ago.

8. Don't threaten divorce.
9. Don't generalize, saying "You always—" and "You never —" and don't name-call ("sex-maniac," "bitch," etc.).

How many in this list did you recognize in the Steffans' fights? How many do you recognize from your own fighting?

Nonverbal Words

Brad Steffan's struggle with Maria's hidden meanings is a classic lesson in communicating. Psychologists are finally beginning to recognize the importance of body language and other clues in communicating. Even direct words are often subject to opposite interpretations. " 'When I use a word,' Humpty-Dumpty said in a rather scornful tone, 'it means just what I choose it to mean—neither more nor less.' "

Albert Mehrabian studied the tangle of communications for a decade and came up with this formula to express the accurate proportions in communications: words alone, 7 percent; tone of voice and inflection, 38 percent. The remaining 55 percent is buried in facial expressions, posture and gestures.[1] Some psychologists say that when a verbal message conflicts with a nonverbal message, the listener always responds to the nonverbal message. This motto expressing the dilemma can be bought in plaque form and hung on your wall:

I KNOW YOU BELIEVE YOU UNDERSTAND
WHAT YOU THINK I SAID,
BUT I AM NOT SURE YOU REALIZE THAT
WHAT YOU HEARD IS NOT WHAT I MEANT

As you read the hidden meanings between Brad and Maria (her looking for encouragement by saying the opposite of what she meant), whom did you side with? Did you think that Brad should have been more understanding or Maria should have been more direct? Are there any parallels in your marriage? If so, have you ever discussed the differences you perceive with your partner?

Lowering Defenses

Paul Tournier: "You well know that beautiful prayer of Francis of Assisi: 'Lord, Grant that I may seek more to understand than to be understood. . . .' It is this new desire which the Holy Spirit awakens in couples and which transforms their marriage. As long as a man is preoccupied primarily with being understood by his wife, he is miserable, overcome with self-pity, the spirit of demanding, and bitter withdrawal. As soon as he becomes preoccupied with understanding her, seeking to understand that which he had not before understood, and with his own wrongdoing in not having understood her, then the direction taken by events begins to change. As soon as a person feels understood, he opens up, and because he lowers his defenses he is also able to make himself better understood." [2]

Rules of the Jungle

Many styles of relating are determined in the first few years of marriage. Dr. Bernard Harnik lists these four common styles: (1) The husband dominates. Harnik says the wife's response will be either to oppose him or to find release elsewhere. (2) The wife dominates. In response, usually the husband develops depressions or retreats behind defenses. (3) Both partners are equally strong and insist on their own rights. The marriage thus becomes a constant struggle. (4) The spouses go their own ways, in sex, money, leisure activities.

As the Christian alternative, Harnik says, "The correct formula can be simply stated: In marriage one may not rule, one serves. If the husband feels stronger then he must submit himself to his wife's possibilities. If the wife is superior to the husband, she should subordinate herself to him so that he doesn't lose his dignity. The strong one thus assumes voluntarily the burdens and problems of the weak one." [3]

Which of Dr. Harnik's styles describes your marriage?

How Christian?

Does a Christian marriage differ from a marriage of unbelievers? In what ways? The consensus of Christian marriage counselors who write on the subject is that three Christian qualities are necessary to make a marriage work:

1. Forgiveness. This must be total and complete, so that the issue of conflict is forgotten and never brought up again.

2. Acceptance. In the same way that Christ's love for us is unconditional and without fine print, acceptance in marriage is all-encompassing.

3. Self-sacrifice. Theodor Bovet says, "True marriage begins

when our self is prepared to die; when I am prepared to sacrifice my own will, my habits, my rights, my personal ambition, my private thoughts, my fantasies. These are real things—it may be reading in bed, weekend climbing, or a brilliant position in society. And it does not necessarily mean renouncing all these or yielding entirely to someone else's caprices but giving up deciding about them by myself, and taking somebody else's views into account. It is not a case any longer of 'I' and 'Thou,' but of 'Us.' " [4]

Are these qualities present in the Steffans' marriage? In yours?

Who's Right?

Brad admits to an intense desire to be proved right. It's a natural desire, a mechanism present in all of us. Only, in marriage, the "who's-right?" argument is one of the biggest blockades to growth. In the first place, many of the disagreements concern matters of taste and cultural training; there is no "right" way to squeeze a toothpaste tube, hold a fork, or decide on a vacation.

But, as Richard Klemer points out, there's an even bigger reason why the "who's-right?" question is futile: It doesn't do any good to know the answer. When Brad stormed and argued and finally forced Maria to admit he was right, it certainly didn't help the relationship. It did not make her love him more. And he did not love her more because she had been defeated. Usually, they both ended up distressed and unhappy. "In most marriages," Klemer concludes, "it is far better to protect the other partner's integrity by allowing him to save face and back off gracefully than it is to score an empty victory by proving you can win the 'who's-right?' arguments." [5]

Looking back, I think the problem was that neither of us had seen a good model of a couple living together. We did not know how to resolve differences as adults, so we acted like children.

CHAPTER EIGHT

Beating History

PETER AND BETH PESTANO

Statistics show that severe marital problems can "run in the family." A person raised in a broken home is more likely to get a divorce. The effects of a smothering, guilt-inspiring mother or a drunken, child-beating father do not mysteriously melt away when the child leaves home and begins a separate life. Those wounds usually leave scars which marriage can aggravate.

Is there a way to avoid the trap? Are people reared in neurotic families condemned to live a neurotic life? That depends on the personality and the extent of the emotional scars. Peter and Beth Pestano, however, stand as an example that where there was dis-ease, healing can take place. The process was long and painful.

Peter's family functioned well until his father decided to move from New Hampshire to Florida, when Peter was seven. Florida offered exciting business opportunities in the construction industry, and Peter's father poured his energies into his business. At his family's expense, he became a compulsive workaholic, and soon had a crew of forty to sixty men working for him.

Peter's father drove a Cadillac and brought elaborate presents for his wife and children, but spent little time with them. Feeling neglected, Peter's mother immersed herself in the "new rich" social life. Soon open conflict broke out. Peter saw his father chase his mother around the house with a broom, shouting obscenities. Once, enraged at the supper table, his father threw a platter of spaghetti at his mother. The children watched in wide-eyed horror as their mother ran from the room and the meat sauce dripped eerily down the wall.

Soon Peter's father had a nervous breakdown. When doctors insisted he find less demanding work, the family moved to Miami and bought a hotel to manage. While living in this hotel, Peter met Beth, his future wife.

Beth came from an even less stable family situation. Her mother died when Beth was eight months old, an event which profoundly affected her father. Her mother, only nineteen, was in a locked bathroom bathing Beth when she suffered a cerebral hemorrhage and collapsed. The bathtub continued filling, and Beth screamed in terror. Beth's father heard her screams, called out to his wife, got no answer, and began pounding on the door. He broke through and found a tragic scene: his wife lying dead in a pool of water and his daughter nearly drowned. He never recovered from that scene.

For four years Beth was shuffled among her father's relatives in California. Then her maternal grandparents drove to California from Detroit and insisted she return with them.

Beth's grandparents had the usual grandparental weakness of spoiling the child. They gave her few rules to follow. As their only form of punishment, they would lecture Beth about what a bad child she was, just like her father had been. Beth soon believed it. She learned to live with a sense of rejection. She could never understand where her father was and why he didn't want her.

When her grandparents moved to Florida, Beth, then a teenager, joined a fast, spoiled-rich set of friends. Many, only thirteen and fourteen, had boats of their own.

Peter and Beth, a most unlikely pair, met in a Miami high school. Peter had been through a dramatic conversion experience in the ninth grade which isolated him from his family. He found a quick new identity in being a "Jesus freak" and was branded as the school's religious weirdo. He stuffed tracts into the vents of lockers and carried a large red Bible on top of his books.

Beth, the aloof pseudosophisticate, was put off by his body odor, bad breath, and lack of manners.

BETH: We dated once in high school, a casual, informal date. I was consciously holding back from all guys then. I had been burned so badly by my father's rejection that I could not trust anyone. Peter interested me for only one reason: at a summer camp during my high school years, I too became a Christian. My conversion was very dramatic and emotional. I knew my life would have to change, but I didn't feel I had the strength to make all the changes. Though somewhat repulsed by Peter's zeal, I was attracted to his confidence in Christ. He was consistent and he seemed to sincerely believe what he said.

PETER: I did believe, but I was also forced into living a double life. My home life was deteriorating further as the hotel setting disrupted my family. We were spread out all over the hotel; I slept in the garage with my brother, and my younger sister slept in the hotel lobby. My mother was cracking under the strain. To survive emotionally, I blocked out as much of home life as I could. I spent little time there, and hung out with my small clique of Christian friends. Strangely, during the same time I was finding a depth and happiness with God. It was divorced from my home life, existing in another realm entirely. I couldn't put the two together. Nevertheless, God was working big changes in me.

BETH: As a high school senior, I rejoiced in my first contact from my father in years. I had received only a few letters from him in my life, though I'd written him dozens. This letter started out with a lie: "Dear Elizabeth: The Post Office must have lost the letters I sent you. Why don't you write?" He had married a Vietnamese girl in St. Louis, had "gotten saved," and was now a Freewill Baptist minister. He invited me to come to California for a visit.

Immediately I began to make plans to visit after high school. My heart beat faster whenever I thought of it. I don't know why I had such a longing for my father, but it had always been there, and I knew I had to go to him.

I flew out the summer after graduation from high school, thirteen years after I'd last seen him. During the six-hour flight I tried to picture what he must be like. Though frightened, inside I was singing. At last I could be with my father and feel his love and acceptance.

Father met me at the airport with his new wife, Lora. She told me she accepted me into her family and wanted me to feel just like I was a child of hers. It was good finally to have a family. The drive from the airport was beautiful. They lived thirty miles east of Los Angeles, and to a Floridian the steep hills around the city were marvels.

My dream world lasted only a few weeks. To commute to my job in Los Angeles, I had to catch a 5:15 A.M. bus to the city. I returned at night after everyone else in the family had eaten. Soon I began noticing that no one in the family was making an effort to accept me. Lora did not try to hide her dislike. She spoke to me curtly and talked against me to my dad. My father couldn't cope. I think I was an embarrassment to him; he couldn't handle the guilt of my mother's death and the way he'd treated me.

It was like the situation in the tale of Cinderella: the family seemed to pull together to shut me out. When I first came, the family would gather in the living room evenings to watch TV. Soon they moved the set into their bedroom and shut the door when they watched it. Their distance made me feel new waves of hurt and rejection.

In high school, if I needed a new dress I'd think nothing of plunking down $50 for a new one. Now I earned $45 a week and spent most of it on food and transportation. Tensions built. Lora condemned me for not helping with housework, but she would never tell me what was expected of me.

In all of California, I had no friends. I felt intense rejection on all sides. I got dressed each day in the darkness, long before sunrise, and then the despair would set in. It followed me all day. I asked God to let me die. I prayed that Lora would love me; nothing happened. Who could I turn to? I lived the hours and days and months mechanically, unthinkingly.

The last two months of my stay in California, we moved in with Dad's mother in Ontario, a suburb of Los Angeles. Dad was leaving to take a church in Nevada and he had to vacate

the parsonage. I still held out hope for some kind of reconciliation up to the day he left. He planned to leave two weeks before
I did, and I yearned for a last-minute, forgive-all scene of hugs
and tears.

On the day he was to leave, I got up early and dressed, listening for the sound of stirring. They knew they had to get up early
to see me off to work. Maybe Dad would surprise me. I put on
my makeup and brushed my hair more slowly than usual, giving
them more time. I dropped the toothpaste tube loudly, in case
they'd overslept.

But no one got up. No one said good-by. I walked out the
door and left a quiet, sleeping house. All the weights of the past
months' rejection jammed together and hit me. I ran to the bus
stop, crying and hurting. (Later I learned Dad had set the alarm
to get up, but Lora had turned it back.)

In the next two weeks, Grandmother tried to explain my
father to me. She had had five different husbands, all through
divorce, and some had tortured Dad. After my mother's death
he had been emotionally disturbed. Once he was picked up for
standing on a street at midnight, beating his head against a
lamppost. Explanations and psychological theories didn't satisfy,
though. I just knew he had rejected me and I was not loved,
and I couldn't take it.

Two weeks later, I made a sad, lonely trip all the way from
California to Florida. It was fitting. Buses are filled with losers,
the rejects. During the hours of riding through barren deserts
and endless plains, deep self-pity sank in.

After eight months' work I had managed to save $200, and
with that, I headed for college.

PETER: While Beth was going through this ordeal in California,
I was traveling with a musical team of teenagers sponsored by
Youth for Christ. Visiting the Near East, Africa, and Southern
Europe had a dynamic effect on me. I was struck with the crying
needs for the gospel.

Meeting missionaries to Moslems who had preached for twenty
years and won only one convert, I became less concerned about
my own petty problems. Even the struggles at home faded in the
background, seeming far away and unimportant. How could I

spend the rest of my life fighting off self-pity and searching for an identity when millions needed the message I could bring?

During the trip I came to grips with who I was and how God could use my life. It was sobering, broadening, mellowing, and mind-expanding. I returned ready to seriously prepare for service to God. And I was convinced I needed a wife and a family of my own.

Beth stood out to me immediately when I arrived on campus. A home girl, I knew her already, and we talked easily. And I sensed a vacuum in Beth. For some reason—a Messiah complex or something—I've always been drawn to impossible situations. A radar sensor inside me picks up people with desperate needs and longings, and I dive into the situation. Beth triggered the sensor.

BETH: At first it seemed Peter was just who I needed. His buoyant optimism was contagious. He would do crazy things: I'd see him between classes doing handstands and cartwheels on the sidewalk. He'd go to a butcher's shop and buy a three-foot-long cow legbone for the school mascot, a basset hound. He never seemed depressed or anxious. Being with him was healing, in an escapist sense. I agreed to start dating him because it seemed safe. Above all, I didn't want to get seriously involved. I had pulled my emotions inside a shell and refused to let anyone break through that shell and touch me. I could not survive another cycle of misplaced trust and rejection.

I had great fears. I thought that whatever it was in me that was so unlovely to cause my own father to reject me—that unloveliness would pop out and destroy any relationship I developed. The pain would return.

Peter and I did silly things on dates, such as going to the children's section of the downtown library and reading Dr. Seuss books. After several hours of hilarity, on the way back to campus that familiar cloud of depression would descend on me. I don't remember choosing; it swooped down and took control of me. Peter could sense it coming. He fought to keep me happy and hold my attention. I withdrew, became sullen, wouldn't talk. Often I'd end a date by saying something like, "Let's make this the last date, Peter. I don't think we should see each other again."

PETER: It was driving me batty. We'd have a fantastic time together, then she would change personalities and unload a bombshell on me. I tried to give her love, not realizing those expressions were causing her fears. She didn't know how to handle love. It was scary for her, because it allowed the possibility of being hurt. I determined to break through.

One night especially, about a month after we'd been dating casually, I could sense a change. I had been singing at a church on Sunday night, and she rode back in my car. It was a chilly October night, and the North Carolina sky was cloudless. I could see a sparkle in her eye. She brightened up, teased me, responded to me, and the evening ended without a big scene. I was hooked from that night on.

Beth brought joy into my life, and that was worth any amount of sadness which came too. I prayed about it, and determined I would not let her hold me off at a distance. I would try to dissolve her fears. I told her the next night, "Beth, I don't know what's happening, but I love you or like you or something, and I'm not going to stop." She froze, told me she couldn't say that, and went into one of her withdrawal moods. She was paranoid for a long time after that night.

BETH: I had no self-perception, really. I never knew why I acted or felt a certain way. I just knew that inside I recoiled when someone got close to me. I worked at shaking Peter loose. I would go up to him between classes, just before an exam, and say curtly, "Peter, I never want to see you again; I think we should break things off." Then I'd take off, running to my dorm, with Peter chasing me, yelling, "Beth, wait, listen to me—"

I was convinced fueling his interest would hurt him even worse. I had seen a movie once about the black widow spider. She spins a web and does an exotic, sensual dance, wooing her tiny male mate. The male approaches cautiously, feebly, stepping on each new strand of the web as if it's a tightrope. The female outweighs him three-to-one and he's frightened, but soon he can't resist. He approaches her, feels her pulsating body, and begins to mount her. Suddenly—often even before he's completed the mating process—she turns on him and violently attacks him, devouring him. I felt I had the black widow's curse.

I believed I would destroy Peter if he got too close. It was a terrible dilemma.

PETER: To this day I don't know why I'm so stubborn and persistent. But Beth's paranoia raised a red flag in front of me and the bull instinct in me said, "Charge!" I refused to be jilted.

Again and again she told me, "I'm no good for you. I will ruin you, drag you down, destroy you."

Whenever I told her I loved her, her response was silence, or something like, "Peter, it won't work. Why don't you give up?" That went on for at least five months.

Spring vacation brought triumph as the months of persistence finally paid off. Home in Florida, in a Dairy Queen parking lot, I asked Beth to marry me. She paused, then she told me she loved me, and accepted my proposal. The impact was indescribable, after so many months of waiting, finally to be accepted. I was ecstatic.

BETH: Even during our engagement period, I was still troubled with rejection. I wondered if I was sucking him into a trap he would regret later. But Peter had proven his love to me. It was as if molecule by molecule his love pushed out my fears and convinced me that he really did want to spend his life with me. I didn't want to admit the truth—self-pity was easier—but Peter's persistence forced me to admit it.

I wrote Father several times about Peter, and he didn't respond. I was about to commit my life to a man, and he didn't give a damn. I felt a lump of sadness and anger whenever I thought of him.

PETER: The honeymoon and summer months after our wedding were delightful. We rented a small cottage in a lime and lemon grove, perfect for a new couple trying to escape the past. Though we weren't getting emotional support from relatives, we had each other. I think those three months can be best described as wound-licking. We had few responsibilities, and we didn't know what to do with our future, but our love was flowing steadily. We rejoiced in each other.

BETH: The big adjustments came raining down when we moved back to North Carolina for Peter to attend school.

We had already accumulated $700 of school debts, and we had no steady income, so I had to stay out of school and work. We found a cheap, junky apartment in a government project. My job barely kept us floating financially, so Peter took on a job selling cookware.

PETER: I was a natural salesman and the product offered a high profit margin, but Beth thought it was beneath me to sell cookware. We had many fights over that. Worse, a $300 set of cookware was stolen out of our locked car one night. I borrowed a deluxe set from my supervisor to use as a display set, and a week later that was stolen too. The bills were mounting up. What I thought would bring in income was actually digging us deeper into debt. I was so desperate and disconsolate that I sat up with a friend for several nights with a shotgun, waiting for the thief to return and steal a planted set of cookware. He did not return.

Beth responded well to the crisis. From the beginning, she nagged me about recurring things she didn't like—selling the cookware, for instance. But when a real crisis came, one that would threaten me and make me vulnerable, she quit the nagging. She would support me when I was weak. She never blamed me and condemned me about the thefts. That was crucial, I think. If a wife attacks a husband when he's down (or vice versa) . . . look out.

The problems which cropped up during that first year kept reappearing for the next two years at least. Looking back, I think the root problem was that neither of us had seen a good model of a couple living together. Beth was raised by elderly grandparents; my parents barely tolerated each other. We had not seen love visibly expressed. We did not know how to resolve differences as adults, so we acted like children.

Beth, especially, played the children games. She had gotten her way by throwing tantrums, so she threw tantrums with me. She screamed, cried, yelled accusations, threw things. It was impossible to reason with her in a tantrum. Once I actually turned her over my knee and spanked her! I was too emotionally caught up in the issues to get perspective and figure out how to help her. Instead I usually stalked out of the house and screeched off in the car. Once again, I sought a survival mechanism, just as I had when faced with my parents' conflict.

Beth was exceedingly verbal. She could let fly tirades of jumbled analysis and personal attacks. When I'd respond with silence, she would beg me to talk back to her, to let it all hang out. But when I did talk and gave her my viewpoint, she couldn't take it. She flashed back to those old feelings of worthlessness and rejection. Many times she knew she was on the wrong side of an argument, but she'd keep defending her position to ridiculous lengths, trying to convince both herself and me that she had a right to what she believed.

I learned silence, not as a game for me, but more to protect her. She simply couldn't handle a give-and-take dialogue. So, I'd wait until she cooled off, when she'd come with a sorrowful apology. Naturally, I kind of enjoyed those apologies, since they acknowledged that I had been right all along. But as they continued, I saw that we were stuck in a rut. We weren't resolving any issues at all. We were merely replaying old tapes. Beth would repeatedly have to admit, "I've been a jerk, Peter, forgive me." Sometimes she'd do it whether she was wrong or not, just to eliminate the conflict.

Every apology was saying to her, "You're wrong. You're never right. You're worthless. You're no good for Peter." It's as if her fears about marriage were self-fulfilling prophecies.

The only thing I knew how to do was keep loving her. When we weren't embroiled in some thick controversy, I piled on the love. I could do that all right; I'd learned to love despite obstacles before we were married.

BETH: Peter did love me. Sometimes people who knew what our life was like say to me, "How in the world did you survive? How did you make it through those tantrums? Why didn't you separate?" It sounds simplistic and maybe a little corny to say it, but I think it's because Peter just won me over with his love. God used his love to melt me. In Ephesians, Paul gives the love command to the husband, and I know from experience why it's so important. I needed love. I soaked it in like a sponge soaking up water. Gradually, it had an effect.

It helped, too, to see Peter live out his Christian life in front of me. He was not hung up with legalism and spiritual clichés.

He knew he had weaknesses and failures, but he shared them with me. I saw him struggle to know God's will and follow Christ's commands. I could see that his motives were pure.

Somehow, Peter never held grudges. After a fight was over, it was over. I didn't have to figure out ways to win back his favor. He accepted me without bitterness.

PETER: I didn't know how to cope with Beth's negative moods, so I tried instead to encourage the positive.

Much of what we went through while I was still in school was a growing up together. Some couples have the idea that they're doomed to repeat the patterns of relating they use during the first months and years. Thank God it's not so. Marriage is open-ended, there's plenty of room for growth. We went through many phases and we relate very differently now than we did those first years. It helped immensely to have some common goals, and that's where I feel Christian marriages have an advantage. Even when we least acted like it, down deep we both wanted to live for God. Knowing that about each other encouraged us.

BETH: One thing about Peter's persistent love—it built up a fierce loyalty in me. When the nights were lonely and filled with doubts, I could always count on his love, and Peter was worth more to me than anything else in life. So I learned to pour myself into meeting his needs. I tried to be cheerful and encouraging and soothing.

When I saw that Peter did not need more pressures from me, I looked for other outlets for my emotions. I worked on friendships, on expanding my base so that I wouldn't weigh Peter down so heavily. He had loved me enough to inject new self-confidence, and I found life could be an adventure instead of a nightmare.

PETER: Beth acted sexier around me, more relaxed. She found friends who affirmed her, and began to trust people other than me. It's hard to remember the clouds that used to hang over our marriage. Sometimes the old problems of Beth's self-worth and rejection have surfaced. Several times I've had to tell her, "Damn your father, Beth; he won't ever be what you want. You've got to expect that!"

I have also learned to accept Beth's need for occasionally blowing up. I can see the reasons for it, and I know it's a temporary thing. She just needs to let off some pressure, and I can't berate her for that. As I've learned to accept her anger, the funny thing is that she blows up less. She feels less threatened.

BETH: Marriage can drive people apart and even push them to emotional sickness. But for us, it was a great healer. God used our love to firm up our personalities and bring new life and vitality to each other.

If you were to ask me when I first started feeling good about our marriage, I'd have to say not until the fourth year. But, after all, we had both brought many years of mistrust and family conflict to each other. It takes time to work through those things. We committed all we knew of ourselves to each other when we got married. That commitment has grown as we've grown. We know ourselves much better now that we're in touch with ourselves, but we follow the same principle: we commit all we know of ourselves to each other.

PETER: Looking back over our romance, it seems strange to me that I could have kept up a loving attitude toward Beth. Why didn't I feel rebuffed and rejected when she first shunned my advances? I don't know the answer. My family did teach me to be stubborn and hard-nosed, and perhaps that helped.

But even more important, I think, was the example of God. God reached out to me and gave me life. That life cost a great deal for him: Jesus' death on the Cross. When the Bible says, "Love your wives as Christ loved the Church and gave himself for it," I think it points to the highest model. *Grace* and *forgiveness* are the two concepts which resonate through the Bible. They're inescapable. They broke through to me personally, and they allowed me to love Beth over the years. What God did for me astounds me. It's been the most powerful motivating factor in my life.

WHAT DO YOU THINK ABOUT THE PESTANOS?

Forget the Past

A new school of psychology, called Reality Therapy, is being pioneered by William Glasser. Reality Therapy teaches you that it doesn't make much difference what kind of background you had. There's really no reason to wallow in your past. Instead, accept yourself now as a free, responsible adult, and decide who you want to be. The Reality Therapy approach is a natural one to apply to marriage situations where one partner comes from a troubled past. A paperback book, *Why Marriage,* by Edward E. Ford, applies this approach specifically to marriage.[1]

When Do We Start?

To introduce his book *Caring Enough to Confront,* David Augsburger penned these lines:

I am responsible for the way I
react to you. You cannot make me angry
unless I choose to be angry. You cannot make
me discouraged, or disgusted, or depressed.
I am free to react in concerned,
understanding ways. . . .
Love ends the blaming games
and gets on to the real questions:
What is the loving, responsible, the truly
respectful thing to do now? Where do we go
from here? When do we start?
If not from here—where?
If not now—when?
Who—if not you and me? [2]

Are You a Psychotherapist?

In their own ways, Peter and Beth adapted to the other's needs. Even in conflict they moved toward each other, not away from each other. Eventually, the approach worked, although, as Beth said, it took four years to convince her she had a good marriage.

Peter dramatically proved the healing power of love. Even when burdens look too big and unwieldy for a couple to carry, love can see them through. A person as scarred as Beth needed someone to listen to her for long periods. She verbally spilled out her pain that had accumulated for years. Peter did not reject her; he loved her, and healing resulted.

Peter showed a defense common to males from emotionally troubled backgrounds: he put on a hard, unemotional front when crises came. Often those of us who see someone with a tough exterior think, "Oh, he's not interested in me. He's independent;

he wants to be left alone." Actually Peter needed someone to push *through* his exterior and find the real person inside. Despite a lot of turbulence and mistakes on both sides, Peter and Beth served as each other's psychotherapist. (Isn't it encouraging to see a couple who made so many mistakes still come out happily married?)

Paul Tournier's words seem to be written as a description of the Pestanos: "How beautiful, how grand and liberating this experience is, when couples learn so to help each other. It is impossible to overemphasize the immense need we have to be really listened to, to be taken seriously, to be understood. The churches have always known this; modern psychology has brought it very much to our attention. At the very heart of all psychotherapy is this type of relationship in which one can tell everything just as a little child may tell all to his mother. No one can develop freely in this world and find a full life without feeling understood by at least one person. Misunderstood, he loses his self-confidence, he loses his faith in life or even in God. He is blocked and he regresses." [3]

In your marriage, are you a psychotherapist or part of the emotional problem?

Magnet or Wedge?

Peter and Beth both testify that their commitment to Christ glued them together. Unfortunately, when one partner thinks he is "more spiritual" than the other, his faith can cause tension. Christianity can cause resentment between partners if one is seen as superior. There are two sure questions about a mature faith, says Dr. Harnik. (1) The mature believer rejects all attempts to justify himself and try to be perfect. He realizes that the main difference between him and the unbeliever is this: the Christian knows he needs help and has admitted it freely to God. (Read Romans and Galatians if you're unconvinced.) There is no room for super-righteous snobbery in the Christian faith. (2) The mature believer has learned to say not only "My God for me" but also "I for my God." [4] On his teen team trip, Peter learned a truth about Christian service: he did not have to be perfect for God to use him. In fact, God used his commitment to service as a part of his own healing.

Dr. Harnik has taken this as his motto: "The greatest demands

John would lie on the hospital bed beside me and, holding each other, we would cry for hours. It was too big, too hard.

CHAPTER NINE

Unwelcome Intruder

JOHN AND CLAUDIA CLAXTON

I have known John Claxton since college days when we worked on the newspaper staff together. We spent many midnight hours in the library basement pasting down headlines and writing photo captions.

John felt comfortable around few people. He was raised overseas, and spent most of his childhood in a boarding school away from his parents. That separation seemed to carve a void in his personality, and his insecurity showed quickly in the way he related to people. He could be talked out of anything. He would fall in love too easily. And with an outer crust of cynicism, he held close relationships at arm's length.

After two years, John moved to Virginia. The stream of letters I got from him there indicated some major changes were afoot. He met a woman who at last seemed the stable, challenging ideal he could live for. His cynicism melted into a reserved attitude of praise and thankfulness. In a short time, John and Claudia Claxton were married.

The Claxtons were obviously in love. A few short months of marriage gave John growth and confidence. Both were genuinely happy to be alive, and glad to spend life with each other.

A year later I received a letter from John. His usually neat handwriting was marked with errors and scratches. He explained,

"Excuse my writing. . . . I guess it shows how I'm fumbling for words. I don't know what to say."

The Claxtons' happy young marriage met a crisis of mammoth proportions. Unlike some of the other crises in this book, this one struck cruelly and suddenly from without. It was not an inherent weakness in their own marriage. It was an unwelcome intruder known as cancer.

JOHN: Claudia was the first person I felt free to open up to. I had always shied from sharing how I really was. There's a book called *Why Am I Afraid To Tell You Who I Am?* and the author answers the title question with this statement, "But if I tell you who I am, you may not like who I am, and it is all that I have." Claudia accepted who I was, including faults, wounds from childhood, fears. She made me want to commit myself to her. She seemed hurt if I didn't. I found no use for the surface cynicism that had kept people at bay.

CLAUDIA: We were married in December, at my home church in Philadelphia. Then we moved to a small cottage apartment on top of a mountain in Virginia.

Our engagement and friendship had been so complete, so thorough, that marriage brought us no big surprises. We had known each other well, and our love proved durable.

Our first year and a half were peaceful, fun times. We never had three-day arguments or called each other names or threatened divorce, as some of our friends did. We looked forward to coming home at the end of a day to see each other.

JOHN: All the warm security, the idyllic love and joy of our relationship were exploded by the events following May 28, exactly one-and-a-half years after our wedding. We were living in Philadelphia by then. Claudia noticed a small, egg-shaped lump between her collarbone and her neck. It appeared overnight, and she saw an M.D. that afternoon. Concerned, he sent her to a surgeon the same evening. The surgeon examined her, seemed worried, and came into the lobby to talk to me. He refused to guess at any causes or give me possible explanations; he just told me it was essential they schedule surgery in five days to perform a biopsy on the lump.

Naturally, we were frightened by the specter of something strange and harmful. But neither of us had much medical knowledge, and we merely waited for the doctor to find the cause and cure it.

I saw the doctor immediately after surgery on June 3. His face was tight and he looked away from me nervously as he talked, but he still refused to conjecture what was wrong. "Wait till tomorrow, John," he said. "Lab tests will be back and I can give you a definite answer."

At the time I was working in a hospital as a chaplain's assistant and had counseled scores of sick and dying patients. The routine of nervous doctors trying to comfort distraught relatives was common to me. Every day when I went to work I saw grief and fear etched on the faces of patients and relatives. But nothing had prepared me for the acid sensation inside me. An unknown was eating at my wife, possibly destroying her. All our joy and happiness, all our future plans were dangerously suspended by the discovery of a tiny lump on Claudia's collarbone.

I did not sleep that night. I fantasized a thousand things the doctor might tell me, from "John, there's nothing to worry about; it was a benign, fluke lump. She'll be home in two days" to "John, I don't know how to say this. Your wife has two weeks to live."

The next day, as promised, the doctor called me into his hospital office. His face showed that my worst fears were closer to reality. "It's Hodgkin's disease," he said quietly, "cancer of the lymph glands." He went on to tell me of recent advances that gave her a 50-percent chance and described medical details of the disease. I sat there stone-faced, hearing what he said, but feeling numbed by the impact of that first sentence. We talked for a few minutes. I had never heard of Hodgkin's disease. He told me major surgery was mandatory. In a week they would cut her open from belly to breast, removing her spleen and doing biopsies on her liver and lymph glands.

The grief hit with blinding force, a paralyzing bolt of lightning. It was if she had received a death warrant. I mentally began preparing for the worst.

CLAUDIA: Fear hit me worse than the grief. You can grieve for a loved one facing death. But when it's *you*—I could only fear.

I read a book by Elisabeth Kübler-Ross, the expert on death, who told of a dying child asked to draw a picture of what he felt like. He drew a huge metal army tank, all grinding gears and protruding guns and massive bulk. At the bottom corner of the picture, inches away from the oncoming tank was a small stick figure holding up a stop sign.

I was that figure. Fear was bearing down on me. I could not stop it. As if outside my body, I watched it move in and take over.

John would lie on the hospital bed beside me, and holding each other, we would cry for hours. We would hardly talk, just hold each other and cry. It was too big, too hard.

Well-meaning friends came in with cheery smiles and handfuls of bright flowers. "Why are you crying?" they'd ask. We would look at them, at each other, and shake our heads. Only we could bear this suffering. We could not pass it around.

A week later, they operated. They removed my spleen, did biopsies of my liver and the lymph nodes around the aorta. The disease had spread through my neck and chest, but had not entered my abdomen. Removing the spleen was a precaution. The doctors hoped by removing it they could deter the growth of the disease, should it spread to my abdomen later.

After surgery the doctors were very encouraged that the disease had not spread into my abdomen. They planned a nine-week schedule of cobalt radiation, which, they said, had some effect 80 percent of the time and tended toward a cure 50 percent of the time.

JOHN: We moved from a small apartment into Claudia's parents' home. She needed the comfort and care of other people around her while I was at work. Her mother cooked all the meals, did the housework, and freed Claudia to rest all day.

She needed the rest. The cobalt was exhausting. She would go to bed at ten o'clock at night and sleep till noon the next day. Twenty minutes at the dinner table with us would exhaust her. The radiation damaged good cells while killing the diseased cells, so her energy was sapped.

For the rest of that summer I continued my internship as chaplain's assistant. I was a mass of emotions. In some ways I could understand far better what my hospital patients were undergoing. In other ways, I wanted to scream at them, "Stop that sniveling, you idiots! You think you've got problems—my wife may be dying right now!"

At first, people around us were very supportive. Church friends would call and visit regularly, praying for us. After the doctors' optimistic report, however, they acted as if everything had been solved.

Together Claudia and I were going through the anger-and-rejection stage. Our anger was against God. It was a familiar anger against a partner you really loved who turned on you. We were rejecting him; we were demanding explanations. "God, why us? Have you teasingly doled out two years of happiness to set us up for this?"

It was the wrestling of Jacob, the agonizing of Job. That threatened some people. They would come in with sweet smiles and read us passages from the Psalms. "I'm sure you're at peace," they would say. I wanted to scream to them. "Hell, no, I'm not at peace. My wife may be dying. You want me to praise God for *that??*"

A few understood. Our pastor would listen to our anger and not try to argue. "Go ahead, get mad," he would say. "God can take it." His attitude was "I don't know what you're going through, but it must really hurt. I don't know what to do but love you, listen to you, and pray."

We needed someone to listen. The worst people were the ones who acted as if nothing was wrong. One lady stood by the bed and joked for a half-hour, trying to cheer us up. No one laughed at her jokes, and the poor fool kept going.

CLAUDIA: Cobalt treatments were very draining. At the start they were twenty minutes long, and they got longer each week. I would go in at noon daily, Monday through Friday. It was a dull, unpleasant routine. I would go to the room, remove my clothes, and stretch out on a cold steel table. I would lie flat on my back, usually nude, and shut my eyes. At first I heard a soft, whirring noise as the operators aimed the machine over the part of the body they wanted treated. Then came a silence which lasted the rest of the session.

I lost all dignity. I began to view my body as an object, something apart from me. Doctors and technicians would come in and move a leg or an arm, or ask me to change positions or hold a breast to one side, and soon I stopped thinking, *This is me they're touching and groping and pulling.* It was something else, apart from me. My body had turned against me.

Lying in the spotless hospital room, surrounded by giant machines that looked like props from *2001,* I had time to think and pray. My fear melted from a fear of something awful and evil bearing down on me. It was more a fear of loss, the possibility of all our joy and happiness dissolving into death. John said eternal life became much more real to him as he watched me suffer; he yearned for a world without suffering. Facing death, though, I did not yearn for eternal life; I wanted to cling to the life I had known and loved.

The cobalt took its toll of me. I was constantly tired, and my throat was raw. Areas of my skin turned dark, and hair at the back of my head began to fall out. At one point they had to suspend treatment when my esophagus swelled so much I could not swallow. I expected to regurgitate everything I ate. Swallowing was a raw, burning chore. I hated eating and drinking.

I always felt weak. This went on for nine long weeks. Worse even than the physical symptoms was the haunting anguish that perhaps it was all in vain.

I went through waves of self-pity. I saw myself as having no worth, since I was a concern and drain on everyone around me. It was always "Poor Claudia," and I began to believe it. John's love and concern were the only strength-giving factors. He would come and sit for hours on my bed, holding my hand, touching my face, telling me he loved me. I believed him.

JOHN: After the cobalt treatments, at the end of the summer, we decided to find our own place to live. Claudia's parents' home had been a welcome retreat, but we needed to cope on our own and begin life together under the new situation. We found a rustic (or, you might say, poorly built) cottage set atop a hill on a twenty-acre estate. When the estate had been a functioning farm, the cottage had been used for a gardener. It had only three rooms, and its construction allowed a steady draft of winter air, but it was quiet and peaceful. We were alone there. The nearest neighbors were hundreds of yards away. To reach the cottage we had to drive down a narrow, twin-rutted dirt road.

Grass around the house was usually waist-high grain. But for us, the cottage was almost symbolic. We needed the peace and solitude it offered. There were no pressures for housekeeping, not in a place with unpainted board walls.

My chaplain internship was over, and I took a job painting houses. The steady rhythm of swishing paint brushes against the side of a house offered much time for thinking and reflecting.

I found myself projecting all the possible alternatives of what might happen. I lived through Claudia's deathbed scene and her funeral and my life afterwards, flushing out the grief, preparing for the worst.

In the process, I found my love for Claudia solidifying and firming. It never crossed my mind to blame her or think of her as a burden. And as I mentally explored all the alternatives, I was absolutely convinced Claudia had to live. I wanted her.

I had seen dying patients in hospitals. It's not like the TV shows and the movies like *Airport*. In the movies couples who have fought for years, in the face of danger, suddenly forget their differences and come together. That's not the way life happens.

When a couple meets a crisis, it's a caricature of their relationship and what's already there. We happened to love each other deeply and had open communication. Therefore the crisis drove us to each other. We were unified. We trusted each other. Doubts and feelings of blame and anger against each other did not come. The crisis of Claudia's illness merely brought to the surface and magnified the feelings already present.

Always the specter of death hung over us, though. We told ourselves intellectually that every couple lives in the face of death; it could swoop down and crumble them in a car on the highway. But that philosophizing did not help. We knew every time Claudia got a sore throat or coughed that, for us, death was much closer.

CLAUDIA: By the fall of the year, our emotions had turned from fear and anger to resignation. We were unwilling to accept the situation, but we begrudgingly acknowledged it was with us. We accepted the inevitability of our changed lives. That fact particularly bothered me, because I had always desired a normal family.

We received another blow. Doctors discovered John was

probably infertile. His sperm count was so low that they doubted any possibility of conception. Questions about my worth kept recurring. Now I did not even have the normal process of motherhood to find my worth and identity. Once again feelings of bitterness and anger crept in. Why were we being picked on? Wouldn't there be any more good news for us? Our lives together had started off with such joy and happiness. Why were we being punished?

Fortunately, we continued to turn toward rather than away from each other. We talked openly when we felt depressed or let down. If I felt like being angry, John didn't try to cover up or talk me out of it. He stayed with me, comforting.

Several years ago I watched a TV movie called *Sunshine,* about a girl dying of bone cancer. It seemed all her doubts and insecurities and fears pounded out spaces between her and her husband. I had those same weak feelings, but John wasn't threatened by them. He had already determined to accept me and love me to the end. So we didn't end up bitterly shouting at each other, and he didn't stomp off looking for sexual fulfillment from some other, healthier woman. He turned to me.

JOHN: Again, as Claudia says, the crisis simply brought to the surface what was already present in our marriage. We had developed patterns of opening up and sharing deep feelings. We had learned to accept sour moods from each other. Thus Claudia's illness became a caricature of our marriage. It speeded our pulse, it heightened our breathing. I'm sure it hurried our growth and maturity. How can a couple prepare for something like we went through? You don't consciously prepare; you just pour your energies into creating a loving nucleus and environment. Only love lasts.

The weight hung over us for at least two years. Claudia had absorbed all the cobalt treatment allowed, so doctors could do nothing but wait. No new signs of the cancer's spreading had cropped up. Still, whenever she'd get a minor sore throat or develop a cough, we'd be thrown back into the cycle of pain and wondering.

I remember a camping trip we took to New England. We wanted badly to get away and forget about hospitals and cobalt machines and intravenous needles. We longed for a week among the trees and hills of New England. But a hacking, raw cough came, and we had to pull off the highway and explain our story all over again to a new batch of doctors, in a strange hospital, hoping they were wise enough to treat us correctly. The doubts and uncertainty traveled with us like a thundercloud.

Psychologically, we received the biggest boost when we found a supportive church. The church was unlike any other we'd been to. Mostly young, inner-city couples attend. The service is not spectacular; it contains the usual prayers and sermon and Scripture readings. But the focus of the service is on worshiping God. So often churches work at entertaining, or capturing interest, or using congregation-oriented gimmicks. This church is constructed to turn attention to God. Through the worship services we began to get our eyes off ourselves and our problems and learned to meet with God.

And the people were fantastic. When we joined, the elders lovingly asked us about all we'd been through and explored with us ways in which they could help us. All of us were crying. We were swept up in their Christian love and support. A weight was lifted from us when we realized other Christians were willing to share our hurts, that our health and psychological well-being was important to them. They prayed for us regularly and encouraged us to share our trials with them.

As we became involved in the church, we found ourselves putting more of our energies into serving. We moved to a rundown area of Philadelphia, a "changing neighborhood" it was called, and began working with tutoring programs. I soon became an elder and accepted a group within the congregation as mine to minister to.

CLAUDIA: I'm sure my struggles with self-worth took a giant infusion from getting involved in the church. I asked the people there not to see me as an invalid. I wanted to minister. And as the focus of my life changed, the depressions gradually lifted.

Helpful people counseled us until we came to the point that we decided to live normally. Yes, I could be dying, but everyone is in some stage of dying. It was no use morbidly dwelling on my increased chances. We really didn't realize how heavy the shroud

over us had been until it was gone. I distinctly remember driving
along in our car one spring and suddenly thinking, *God is good!
He loves us!* He had enriched our lives in so many ways.

The crowning point of God's goodness came in the shape of a
squirming, eight-pound double miracle. Remember, doctors had
cautioned me that childbearing might be impossible, and had
ruled John sterile. But suddenly I was delightfully, hilariously
pregnant. The baby came without serious complications. He was
perfect. No dreaded birth defects or problems.*

Not long ago we held a baptism for our young son. We named
him Nathaniel, "gift of God." My father performed the baptism,
and it seemed to put a seal on the goodness God had showered
on us. After months of agony and doubting, we had suddenly
burst into the sunshine of God's blessing. It was a terribly moving experience.

The real gift does go deeper than a baby and the prospects of
my living a fairly normal life. The gift that has meant most to
us is the gift of being able to share life. Marriage is under attack
and is corroding in a lot of areas. But God proved to us: together
we can be stronger than apart. His love spread through us to
each other and pulled us through.

WHAT DO YOU THINK ABOUT THE CLAXTONS?

Tough Love

Hopefully, few of you will face such suffering and fear in the
first years of your marriage. But life is full of pain, and eventually
we will all encounter heavy grief and sadness. What kind of love
can help make that experience a shared, unifying experience—
not a divisive one? The Claxtons taught me these essentials about
love tough enough to survive tragedy:

1. *Unconditional love.* It cannot be based on performance.
Balanced children are usually raised in homes where parents

---

*Six months later, the Claxtons discovered their child had suffered
damage to his muscle tone and his mental learning may be impaired.
Doctors believe this was unrelated to Claudia's disease. Extent of his
disability is still unknown.

make them feel loved and accepted just because they belong, not because of their behavior or performance.

If you don't communicate to your marriage partner that your love is unconditional, he may harbor a lurking fear that love will be taken away if the partner does not meet expectations. When tragedy hit, Claudia naturally had feelings of "What good am I to John? I am merely a burden. I am ruining our young love and happiness." John's mature, accepting love overcame those fears.

2. *Transparent love.* By transparent, I mean love strong enough to allow you to be absolutely transparent with your partner. At first, John was afraid to reveal who he was because Claudia might reject him. But he learned that she would never reject him, so he felt free to share his deepest feelings with her.

Paul Tournier tells of one woman whose mother gave her this advice: "Don't tell your husband everything; to maintain her prestige and keep her husband's love, a woman must retain a certain mystery for him." Tournier comments, "What a mistake! It fails to recognize the meaning of marriage and the meaning of love. Transparency is the law of marriage and the couple must strive for it untiringly at the cost of confessions which are always new and sometimes very hard." [1]

In the grief process, Claudia met many people who misunderstood her, who could not fathom the experience. But she felt free to share her deep fears with John, and he became her comforting supporter.

3. *Complementary love.* If either John or Claudia had dominated the other, grief would have hit much harder. If Claudia had dominated and built up resentment, it would have been difficult for John to feel empathy for her condition. If John had dominated Claudia before the illness, she might have felt more rejected and worthless while she was sick.

Instead, the Claxtons learned to complement each other. Where one was weak, the other brought strength. Where one had a need, the other tried to shore it up. That early pattern later allowed John to say of a tragic situation: "The crisis simply brought to the surface what was already present in our marriage."

4. *Stored-up love.* John will tell you the best way to prepare for the bad times is to love fully in the good times. It does no good to fearfully and anxiously dread impending tragedies. What is important is to love freely, celebrate life, and have fun when

health is with you. What does a dying person regret? Usually not having lived fully enough. Determine to fill your marriage with a reservoir of happiness and mutuality.

Getting Ready

You can defuse some explosive situations by anticipating adjustments. Assume that such events as moving, job changes, death of relatives, and birth of children will be momentous, disruptive events. Talk about them in advance. Decide how you differ in your attitudes toward these changes. And, be sure to have some financial safety-valve for a crisis such as the Claxtons faced. Many young couples have trimmed health insurance from the budget as an unnecessary expense. If the Claxtons had not been insured, they could be paying medical bills the rest of their lives.

Never Alone

What can you offer a partner under duress? Consider Howard Thurman's summary:

> I know I cannot enter all you feel
> Nor bear with you the burden of your pain.
> I can but offer what my love does give:
> The strength of caring. . . .
> This I do in quiet ways
> That on your lonely path
> You may not walk alone.[2]

Brief Classic

C. S. Lewis has tenderly and brilliantly captured the human response of grief in his brief book *A Grief Observed*. With anger, pain, and humiliation, he thrashes through the enigma of his wife's death. They married when he was in his sixties, and they had a few brief years of ecstasy before her cruel death. In the book he also confronts the theological problems of "Why is God letting this happen?" but in a human, emotional way. I strongly recommend this sixty-page classic (Seabury Press).

Crown of Thorns

A tragedy like the one John Claxton faced can offer the best opportunity for expressing the ideal of marital love, as seen in the passage beginning with Ephesians 5:25. Listen to C. S. Lewis' interpretation of that passage. "Christian writers have sometimes spoken of the husband's headship with a complacency to make the blood run cold. We must go back to our Bibles. The husband is the head of the wife just so far as he is to her what Christ is to the church. He is to love her as Christ loved the church—read on—*and gave his life for her*. This headship, then, is most fully embodied not in the husband we should all wish to be but in him whose marriage is most like a crucifixion; whose wife receives most and gives least, is most unworthy of him, is—in her own mere nature—least loveable. For the church has no beauty but what the Bridegroom gives her; he does not find, but makes her lovely.

"The Chrism of this terrible coronation is to be seen not in the joys of any man's marriage but in its sorrows, in the sickness and sufferings of a good wife or the faults of a bad one, in his unwearying (never paraded) care or in his inexhaustible forgiveness: forgiveness, not acquiescence. As Christ sees in the flawed, proud, fanatical or lukewarm church on earth that Bride who will one day be without spot or wrinkle and labours to produce the latter, so the husband whose headship is Christ-like (and he is allowed no other sort) never despairs." [3]

In marriage we are tiptoeing through a field of land mines on the way to paradise.

CHAPTER TEN

A Goal Too High

I could not end this book without reporting the changes in attitudes and perspectives which researching it has effected in me. As I interviewed close friends for each chapter, it was an emotional experience to climb inside the secret places of their marriage and discover areas usually sealed off from others. Some revealed raw edges of conflict which may never be resolved. Others gladly shared keys of happy living. I felt as if I were standing on the sidelines watching nine marriages—living organisms—sliding unrelentingly toward ruin or toward bliss.

Yet comparatively, these nine marriages are marriages that are working; I interviewed none on the brink of divorce or separation. The widest gaps between partners I interviewed would seem mere cracks alongside those in many American marriages.

Later, as I studied dozens of books written by marriage experts, I noticed a similarity among them. Almost all of them opened with a lead like this: "Marriage is an institution under attack today. Divorce rates are skyrocketing. Just decades ago only one of seven marriages ended in divorce; now it's one of every three or four. In some states divorces outnumber marriages.

"Can the institution withstand these attacks? The pressures on marriage are greater now than they've ever been."

The question is not idle. If you scan history, you'll note we place greater demands and expectations on marriage now than at any other period. Something unique has appeared. Not only must marriage satisfy a person's needs for genital sexuality, now it is being asked to supply needs for comradeship and partnership as well. Instead of a helpmate and mother to a man's children, a wife is now seen as a sexual, emotional, and intellectual colleague. She must meet her husband on all those levels; in turn he must satisfy her ballooning expectations. Added to this burden is the weight of ideals our romanticizing culture excites in us. No wonder many marriages cannot bear the strain.

Is our ideal of marriage too exalted? Is it humanly possible to forge a unity where two people do become one—a separate, cooperative identity? The ideal runs counter to the most basic human tendencies. The fundamental human need, says John Powell, is "a true and deep love of self, a genuine and joyful self-acceptance, an authentic self-esteem, which result in an interior sense of celebration: 'It's good to be me. . . . I am very happy to be me!' " [1] I must learn to enjoy being myself, and not want to be anyone else. Paradoxically, marriage calls us to transcend that fundamental human need and to lose ourselves in another person.

From our toddler years we learn to protect ourselves. If someone criticizes us, we cannot help recoiling like a rattlesnake. We flush with anger. We want to lash out in revenge. Our self must be protected at all costs. Marriage calls us to lower those barriers and expose our nakedness to another person. There are no secrets.

We are taught to love and cherish our freedom; we store up pulses of freedom until adolescence, then explode into adulthood. But marriage calls us to abandon freedom and choose a new bondage, where the needs of the mate take precedence over our own.

Does marriage ask too much? Is the goal too exalted for the fallen man? My answer is precisely yes, in the same way the goal of the Christian life is too exalted for man. The way Christ laid out—"Be ye perfect"—is unreachable; yet it is a goal we cannot forsake.

The imagery of the family is locked into Scripture from Genesis onward. I believe God created the family as the central carrier of the godly value system. Consider the other institutions

in this world: government, corporations, schools, armies. All
are based on status and competition. You rise in them by proving your greater worth. Your business succeeds when you prove
your product is better and you outsell the competition. In the
Army, your worth is determined by the stripes on the sleeve.
Guys with few stripes take orders. Guys with many stripes give
orders and live in plusher quarters. The entire world system is
built on competition, on the struggle to be the fittest.

Against this background, God carves out a unit called the
family, where worth is determined by the mere chance of birth.
A moron son has as much worth as a genius; his acceptance in
the family is not questioned. He deserves love simply because he
was born and bears the family name.

The prodigal son who squanders his father's riches is wel-
comed as eagerly as his older brother who followed all the rules.
(And the lesson of the older brother is the lesson of one who
tries to inject the world's value system into the family, demanding
that behavior determine worth.)

The family is God's great metaphor for his own relationship
with humans. Jesus pronounced that God would adopt us as
sons, not as slaves. We inherit the privileges of sonship. We
are accepted and forgiven and loved because we are sons.

What does this have to do with a young couple who are groping through their first five years together? Everything. It sets
the ideal of marriage squarely in the midst of God's value system,
not the world's. It allows the creation of a cocoon of love and
acceptance which is God-based. God becomes the Source around
which a successful marriage orbits. As I reflect on the lessons
taught by my friends' marriages, it amazes me that their experience proves the need for the kind of love God offers.

Numerous couples mentioned to me the passage in Ephesians
5 which presents Christ's example as the model for husband-to-
wife love. For a marriage to work, each partner must count the
other more important than himself, not grasping at his "rights,"
but seeking ways to fulfill the other.

St. Francis prayed, "Grant that I may not so much seek to be
consoled, as to console; not so much to be loved, as to love. For
it is in giving that we receive, it is in pardoning that we are
pardoned, it is in dying that we are born again to eternal life."

If husband and wife can both maintain that spirit, a marriage will work.

Other couples ranked fidelity as the crucial quality of love in marriage. Again, God gives the perfect model. The Old Testament rings with his stubborn, long-suffering fidelity to rebellious Israel. In the Book of Hosea, God chose an incredible human allegory. He demonstrated that his fidelity was so great it could forgive gross adultery.

Again and again, my friends mentioned their natural human tendency to change and manipulate what they didn't like. Change is the battleground of the first five years of marriage. We want to control the other person, squeeze him into our mold and personality. We want to seize his freedom. In contrast, God valued freedom so much he built into every person the ability to reject him. He refuses to manipulate.

Does it do any good to spiritualize about how marriage is like the Christian life and how true love is God's love? Only if you believe marriage can be a crucial settlement in God's Kingdom. It is exalted, not because it is so different from the rest of life, but because it allows us a frontier to practice God's value system, so that we may derive strength to present that system to the rest of the world.

The exalted nature of marriage assures us that it will contain strife and conflict. In marriage we are tiptoeing through a field of land mines on the way to paradise. If we succeed, and two do become one—there is no more incredible human relationship.

Dostoevski once declared, "I ponder, 'what is hell'? I maintain it is the suffering of being unable to love." [2] What, then, does that make heaven?

APPENDIX

Once you've survived the first five years, what next?

As an encouragement to all of us who are still toddlers in the marriage pilgrimage, I'm including interviews with two of the happiest Christian couples I've known. Their names have popped up regularly throughout this book, for their advice on marriage is invaluable.

Charlie and Martha Shedd have proven their success in many areas. They took a church with fifty members in Houston and led it to a membership of three thousand. Working together on a dozen books, *Letters to Karen, Letters to Philip, The Stork is Dead, The Fat Is in Your Head,* the Shedds have helped scores of thousands of readers.

Dr. Paul and the late Mme. Nellie Tournier differ from the Shedds in temperament, style, and nationality, but their success has been just as phenomenal. Paul Tournier is a major force in Christian counseling. *The Adventure of Living, The Meaning of Persons, To Understand Each Other* and many other books have uniquely blended his professional expertise and warm empathy.

Both these couples bared themselves in the following interviews. The interview with the Shedds was conducted by editors of *The Wittenburg Door,* a magazine for Christian youth workers; the interview with the Tourniers was conducted by editors of *Faith at Work* Magazine in Europe.

The Shedds and Tourniers bring hope: husband and wife together, they have made the institution of marriage succeed.

CHARLIE AND MARTHA SHEDD:
WHY OUR MARRIAGE WORKS SO WELL

CHARLIE: Martha and I were recently asked where we think marriage is in the Christian church today. I am sorry to report we don't think more than 10 percent of marriages in America are anywhere near maximum. Maybe closer to 5 percent, mostly because people aren't honest with each other. They've never learned to live in the grace of God. They've never extended each other the mercy of the Lord. So, they live behind masks and move behind a façade in everything they do. As a consequence, they go through life looking for someplace to relate.

MARTHA: I think that's basically it—a matter of communication, honest communication. People don't take time for depth communication so they can be friends and have a good time.

It's difficult to begin to pull a marriage back together after five, maybe ten years of mediocrity. But, set up some goals together. Everybody has twenty-four hours a day, and you can decide what to do with it. Charlie and I decided long ago we would go out once a week alone on a date. We've stuck with that and it's meant everything to our marriage. It also means a lot to the kids. They love it. Saturday, they send us out if we haven't been out through the week.

CHARLIE: We didn't begin this right from the start of our marriage so we were pretty estranged from each other. Amazing thing. We'd gone together a long time so we felt we knew each other as well as two people can know each other. Yet when we got married we began to withdraw from each other.

Martha was raised in a home where she had picked up a shyness, an inferiority complex. I was very outgoing: a slam-bang kind of guy, a phony.

So since we were becoming estranged from each other and we didn't want this estrangement, we decided to do something about it. We committed ourselves to (a) time with each other, (b) total honesty, (c) prayer. That's what we're really pushing for marriage: prayer! If we can get a couple to commit themselves for a duet of prayer, they can build a good marriage. Once they begin relating to the Lord, then their relationship grows in depth.

If the two of you can't seem to pray together out loud, try what we did. We began our prayers in silence.

MARTHA: We have a favorite place where we sit down—a rocking love seat in our living room. We hold hands and talk over the things we want to pray about. Anything that is troubling us or something we're grateful for. Then we pray silently. We started this way and we still do it. Anybody can do that. Then we say the Lord's Prayer or "Amen" when we think we've gotten through.

CHARLIE: We have four goals at our house for a praying home.

MARTHA: One goal is that each of us has a quiet time every day. Charlie and I get up early and we have our quiet time . . . reading the Bible or inspirational books. This is our time of meditation. Another goal in our family is that everybody prays for everybody else every day. (There are thirteen now, including in-laws and grandchildren.) Third, we pray together as husband and wife. And our final goal is family devotions. We try to do that every day and we succeed most of the time, maybe 75 percent. It's a real celebration time.

CHARLIE: Back to the quiet time—study is a big part of our prayer life. We study materials which we share with each other. Once in a while we read a book together. Martha reads to me or I read to her. We do this sometimes when we're in the car. But more often we read alone in our quiet time. We read the Bible. Martha will mark with one color and I mark with another. Then we discuss what we read. "I came on this verse, honey, and it said this to me. What do you think?"

We also read self-help psychology. We started out with surface material, but we've gotten now where we read straight psychiatry. Depth stuff.

We read material of this kind and as we read we use certain signals—an arrow if it convicts us, a candle for new light, a star if it's important. We also underline.

When I find some crazy part of me coming to the surface, I write "Me" in the column. Then I discuss this with Martha. She writes "Me" in her column, and we talk about that. (One thing we try to avoid is demeaning each other's dignity. I never write "Martha" in the column and she never writes "Charlie.")

In this way we are researching each other all the time. I guess you could say we're being each other's psychiatrists. This could be very dangerous for a couple unless they are in tune, honest, praying.

Some forms of public prayer seem to inhibit communication and put people behind a façade or mask, so we find ourselves making speeches to each other. That kind of prayer only adds to the problems of communication in marriage. The vocal prayer Martha and I share together now first had to be learned in silence. It was hard for us to learn this truth. Prayer is not telling God how *we* want it. Real prayer is God telling us how *he* wants it.

MARTHA: In our fast-paced, go-go-go culture a couple must be disciplined to survive in communication. In fact, we think discipline is all-important, but our prayer life isn't rigid. It's a relaxed discipline. And it's something we have a good time at—like our family devotions.

CHARLIE: Just to float into this kind of communion life because you're so in tune with each other is not our experience. There may be people who do that, but we don't know them.

A great thing about a great prayer life is the kind of sex life it leads to. Without question Martha and I found that it was after we began praying together that our sex life really took off. And, praise the Lord, we don't know of another couple with as potent and vibrant a sex life as Charlie and Martha Shedd!

Since we don't know another couple with a better prayer life, do you think they go together? We think they do.

We also think it could be dangerous for a couple, if they're engaged and a couple of years away from marriage, to begin praying together. Could lead to sex. It's a fact: a spiritual union can lead to physical union.

We're sixty years old and nobody we've ever talked to has a sex life like ours. For us it's like this—sex is a gift of God and the closer we draw to the Lord the more he turns us on all over.

MARTHA: I agree 100 percent!

CHARLIE: Wouldn't it be too bad for me if she didn't! . . .

Couples who are having problems relating to each other sexually probably need to build up their prayer life. At least, it's a good place to begin. Of course, there are cases where it's physical. And here's a sad note. Often the problem is on the male side. In every group we get into we meet some males who have lost their ability or their interest. So there's a very frustrated female here. This guy needs help. Help from a psychologist, a psychiatrist, a counselor. Some men are sex idiots. They don't know thing one when it comes to turning a woman on. Really. But the guy who knows what he's doing can sit across the room, never lay a hand on his woman, and get her so excited she's ready. Of course this takes a man with imagination, plus it takes a lot of understanding of what the female is. But he can learn it. And most men don't take the time or make the effort to learn it. That's why I say most of the sex problems I see are the man's fault.

MARTHA: Like Charlie says, it takes time and work and communication and honesty to turn a woman on. Plus talk during the sex act. Willingness to say "I like this" or "I'd like that better right now."

CHARLIE: It's a matter of learning from your spouse—communicating and finding out what turns her on. Plus learning from people who know what they're doing. One of my favorite books on this particular question is a book called *Letters to Philip.* (I happened to write it.) But I don't see how any man could read *Letters to Philip* without understanding that sex to a woman is not an act, not a happening, it's a creation. It's a twenty-year warmup.

MARTHA: It's too bad so many people consider men and women in the ministry to have less sexuality than the average person. If a pastor looks at a girl in a bikini and smiles, some people question his spirituality. I feel if Charlie doesn't keep on responding to girls in bikinis, he's not going to be much good for me.

CHARLIE: Martha is superb at getting me to evaluate the various arrangements of molecules. We live on a beach and watch these girls go by in bikinis and she very often will say to me, "What do you think about this one?" or "Which of those three do you like?"

But, to get back to the church, I think it has put a shamey-shamey on sex. Because this is true, the churchman is supposed to be above sexual feelings. The church needs to say sex is beautiful because it's from the Lord. He thought it into being. Enjoy it.

A man can look at other women in lust. He can plan and connive, and let his mind get carried away. Or he can enjoy sex because it's God's gift.

MARTHA: It was difficult at first to see Charlie looking at other women, and we did struggle with it for a while. The jealousy problem was an awful one. But I think this can be answered through prayer. I know the beggest step was when I finally got the feeling that I was important to the Lord, that he loved me, that he made me sexual too.

CHARLIE: Here's one of the most beautiful things which ever happened in our relationship. One day early in our marriage Martha told me, "I'm never again going to be jealous, Charlie. I've turned that over to the Lord, and the answer I got was that my love for you is strong enough for anything. So if you do ever have intercourse with another woman, come home and tell me. We'll talk about, we'll pray about it, and I'll still love you."

Then she said this one thing further—"If you ever are unfaithful, remember I'm in the wings loving you." Beautiful way to ruin a man's fantasies, isn't it? And I have never one time been unfaithful to Martha. Not because *I'm* good, but because *she* is. This is "Grace." Living Grace.

She's standing in the free, unmerited favor of God. No, every marriage isn't ready for that. We wouldn't recommend that for everybody. But it's a true story of what happened in the life of one couple.

MARTHA: Sometimes a couple has been brought up in a church which feels a lot of things are taboo for Christians—oral sex, etc. We don't think there's anything a Christian couple couldn't do. If it isn't harmful to either one physically, emotionally, mentally, we think the more uninhibited, the better.

CHARLIE: The more uninhibited, the more likely we will reach the potential God wants us to reach. One of the tragedies of sex in couples we've worked with is that many people have so little imagination. Recently, browsing in a bookstore, we found a book on 147 different positions for intercourse. That's twice as many as the Japanese say there are. So we bought it and when we got home we discovered our favorite position wasn't even in there. We thought that was some kind of fun.

MARTHA: People get in a rut too on the time and place for intercourse. A couple visited us not long ago who only had intercourse on Saturday night. Imagine. We think it's good any time, any day, and almost any way.

CHARLIE: I was brought up, like most boys, I think, to believe that unless a man can put his wife into orbit every time they have intercourse, he's a failure. But one of the big forward steps in our sex life came when Martha convinced me that sometimes she was satisfied to enjoy my enjoying her.

Psychologists say what's important is that you both get what you need. It was a beautiful moment in our marriage when I finally got this through my thick skull. When a woman can convince her man "I just want to be a missionary to your needs tonight," this is beautiful.

MARTHA: Here again we're back to prayer. We don't think anyone is going to have that kind of relationship until they learn how to pray. We deliberately set priorities. The church in Houston had 55 members when we went there and over 3,000 when we left. Charlie wrote eight books in that time. During this time, we decided (a) God first, (b) then our marriage, (c) then our children. It's also when we decided on one night out each week. We also had one night for family night with the children, and this was the best witness Charlie gave in that church. I know of marriages which were saved and homes made happier because they knew their preacher wasn't coming out to a committee meeting or a social meeting on the nights set aside for his wife and children. Home, family, marriage, prayer, great sex, fun living together can be had. We think that's how God intended it.

(Adapted by permission from *The Wittenburg Door,* copyright © 1975 by Youth Specialties, 861 Sixth Avenue, Suite 411, San Diego, California 92101.)

PAUL AND NELLIE TOURNIER:
HOW WE HANDLED DIFFERENCES IN OUR MARRIAGE

DR. TOURNIER: It is our conviction that God has a plan for every person, and that the meaning of life is to seek God's will in order to carry out this plan.

If He has a plan for me and a plan for Nellie, then it follows that He must have a plan for both of us. But inevitably each of us sees God from his own point of view, so that the search for God can become a source of real harmonization between the two of us.

That is not easy. There are Christians who say, "Only believe, and problems disappear." However, that is not what we've found, and indeed we feel that the hard work which the difficulties of life make of the search for God has caused us to mature.

The will of God is not easy to know. The most terrible wars have been religious wars, precisely because both sides were convinced that God was on their side. I've also seen religious wars in families. How tragic it is to see the cruelty with which a believer can treat his spouse! A certain pastor who brought his sick wife to me remarked, "You see, Doctor, I have the Holy Spirit and she doesn't." I immediately thought, *That attitude in itself would be enough to make his wife sick!* If he did have the Holy Spirit, the Spirit could tell him to rethink his attitudes!

We laugh at such an extreme example, but all of us tend to think that God is of our opinion rather than our neighbor's. Little by little I have learned that God speaks to everybody—men and women, adults and children, blacks and whites, the rich and the poor. To discover the will of God, you must listen to Him in all men. Of course I prefer to have God speak directly to me, rather than through my wife, and yet in truly seeking His will I must be persuaded that He speaks as much through her as through me; to her as much as to me.

Then God becomes a voice which is neither my voice nor her voice, but one which can unite us. Neither my wife nor I possesses God. We seek Him together, and to seek Him together there must be oneness between us. Conjugal communion, even in the best of marriages, is difficult.

My wife intimidates me, even after more than 40 years of marriage. And timidity is a real hindrance to human encounter. At the moment I am working on a book, and when Nellie says, "Would you like to read a bit of it to me?" I'm intimidated. I could read the manuscript to a thousand persons with less effort than it takes to read her a single passage. How important it is to be able to feel free and relaxed with each other!

MME. TOURNIER: When Paul asked me to marry him, what an explosion in my life! He was a great intellectual, and I was not even a good student. All through my youth I had considered Tournier far above other people. I certainly did not think of myself as his equal.

DR. TOURNIER: I have tried to give her good reasons to help her find a sense of equality: psychological, theological, philosophical, etc. The more reasons I gave, the more she felt inferior to me. Even in matters of faith this was a difficulty. We wanted to make ours a Christian home, so from time to time we took the Bible and I read from it. Then I commented on the Scripture passage and my wife listened, passive and silent. It wasn't very lively, and often we would give up trying.

Then we would say, "No; we must have devotions together," and the whole thing would begin again. I played preacher and Nellie was my flock.

MME. TOURNIER: I clearly sensed that if I could get to the point where I could pray just once in my husband's presence, I would be freed from my feelings of inferiority. Finally I did so by selecting a hymn and praying the words. Later I was able to pray using words of my own.

DR. TOURNIER: We had a long way to go to become a real couple. I lived in the intellectual world, and she had the simplicity of faith. Slowly, we were able to bring together a union of my complexity and her simplicity. Such a union is extremely important for simplicity without thought turns maudlin, while religious thought without faith's simplicity becomes empty theology.

A decisive event on the path we travelled turned out to be our discovery of silence. In 1932 I met a man who told me of the importance silent meditation played in his life. The next day I attempted an hour of silent meditation in God's presence. At the same time, unknown to me, my wife was trying the same thing.

Neither of us dared speak of this experiment to the other. When at last we admitted what we were doing, we began to wait upon God silently together.

Both of us felt ill at ease. During those periods of meditation it would have been easy for me to fall back into my pattern of abstract thought, but there was no question of that for the subject was my life and what God was saying to me, personally, about it. As verbalizing had always been an obstacle between Nellie and me, silence became for us an open door.

MME. TOURNIER: Once when I said something to my husband which I had sensed during our common silence, he began to enlarge on it. I found the strength to say, "I'm talking now about something I feel God is trying to bring us to understand. There's no need for you to embroider it."

DR. TOURNIER: Our temperaments are quite different, and a lot of work had to be done in order for our viewpoints to converge. This convergence is the work of God in our marriage.

I'm an optimist and she a pessimist. She thinks of every difficulty, misfortune and catastrophe that might happen, and I cannot promise her that such things will not happen. But God is neither optimist nor pessimist. The search for Him leads one beyond his own personality and temperament to a path that is neither optimism nor pessimism.

Another difference between us is that I tend to take the stance of a man who knows no fear, while Nellie is of a rather fearful nature.

One night our son had gone somewhere in the car and did not return when expected. Both of us were very worried, and suddenly I said to Nellie, "I'm just as upset as you are, though I try to hide it."

She replied, "That makes me feel better," for she was no longer alone in her fear.

Husband and wife tend to accentuate their attitudes in a delicate balance of oppositions. Each becomes a counterweight to the other. If one shows fear, the other hides it. But in fact all of us are divided between fear and courage. The separation, the frontier, is not between the two spouses, but in each of us.

Still another difference we have had is our attitude toward money. I don't like to earn but I love to spend. My wife is quite content for me to earn, but she doesn't like to spend. Again, we had to converge and find a common meeting ground.

MME. TOURNIER: The man who raised Paul—he was an orphan and his uncle cared for him—came to me one day and said, "The Tourniers have always spent everything. But I know that in your family you have been taught to count the pennies. I want you to be minister of finance in this household."

This was difficult to suggest to my husband, but because we had those periods of silent meditation, I was able to bring it up. Thereafter he turned over to me all the money he earned, and together we decided what to do with it.

DR. TOURNIER: With the children my wife was rather strict, and I very easygoing. We were in fact reacting to each other. One day during meditation I had this thought: *I'm really leaving the whole burden for her to carry. I have to be more aware of my responsibilities, stricter with my children.* Whereupon my wife said, "Then I can be less strict!"

Then there are the severe trials of life.

In 1937 we had an automobile accident. I was driving and my uncle, the man who raised me, was killed. Immediately I realized that something terrible and irrevocable had happened. It could never be undone; all I could do was take my suffering to the foot of the Cross and there be forgiven. There was no legal guilt, but I could not rid myself of the feeling of guilt until I prayed and placed it in God's hands.

MME. TOURNIER: I was injured in that accident and hospitalized. During my convalescence and for several months afterward I suffered the pain of knowing that Paul had killed his uncle—it was not his fault, but the death was a fact. At last I turned to my pastor, who had stood by me throughout the ordeal. He said everything humanly possible to bring me comfort, but none of it spoke to my need. Only as I was leaving did he ask, "Did Christ die on the Cross for a few things or for everything?"

A few nights before Christmas I awakened during the night and heard the word *everything*. I was released. When I thought about the accident, the pain was gone.

DR. TOURNIER: If it is true that God has a plan for us, then there mùst be turning points, moments when we must follow in the direction He seems to indicate.

In 1936 we reached such a turning point. It seemed to me that God wanted me to leave medical practice for evangelism. I began to be less absorbed by my life as a doctor, which seemed commonplace compared to the life of an evangelist. I was very enthusiastic about the new prospect, but Nellie was not at all convinced. Again, our different temperaments played their part: I am an adventurer, and she is prudence itself.

What do a husband and wife do when they are seeking to follow God's will but can't agree on what that is? The only thing to do is wait until God gives more light.

For several months we went through a very difficult period. One day when we were fed up with our endless discussions I actually felt despair. But we kept on waiting and hoping.

There were also financial implications to the problem: giving up my medical practice meant giving up job security.

MME. TOURNIER: I had "charming" friends, even relatives, who said to me, "If you go along with that scheme, don't count on us for help." But our younger son, not yet ten years old at the time, said one day, "Mother, I'll soon be able to go out and earn a living."

At last I really sensed that my husband had received a call to become an evangelist, while remaining in his practice. So I asked a young pastor if I could pray in his presence to accept the prospect that my husband fulfill God's will by becoming a doctor-evangelist.

DR. TOURNIER: When I realized that God did not want me to leave medical practice but to put my faith to work in it, I knew it would be necessary to inaugurate a new kind of medicine. I would consecrate myself to the task of discovering to what degree one's spiritual life could influence his health. None of my close friends understood what I was trying to do. I was alone, with only my wife's real understanding.

How I wanted some direct bits of advice from God, but I had only three ideas: to re-read a certain book in order to find out whether there were answers to those questions for which medicine has no answer; to talk things over with six colleagues; and to write a letter to my clients explaining that now I would concern myself with the influence of spiritual life on health.

We went away for two weeks, still waiting for God to give me additional inspiration. It never came, and at last I understood that I must begin with the ideas I had, and God would supply others later.

During all the succeeding years our periods of meditation have been the source of the whole direction my professional life has taken. I had to resolve practical questions: how to organize my time, for instance. With patients to see, meetings to attend, books to write, speeches to give, there were always conflicts over how to budget my time. Which invitation should I accept? Which article should I decline to write? We always took up such questions together in meditation.

Now that I'm getting old and must reduce my activities, there are new problems, and each time the working together of two temperaments is necessary. Together we seek the right path according to God's will.

The path is different for each person, and for each couple. Don't try to imitate us; follow your own path. Perhaps it will be to speak rather than remain silent.

What counts is the search for God. Sometimes there are answers. Sometimes you have the definite conviction that God is asking something precise of you. But very often there is only silence, with no answer. Only long afterwards do you discover that God's plan has been carried out without your knowing it was done, and that you have been guided without realizing it.

My wife and I thank God for the way He had led us and for all He has given us. The most important thing is not to have received such-and-such an order, because we're often mistaken about that. No, the most important thing is to enter more and more into intimacy, so that our intimacy as a couple is deepened by our intimacy with God.

(Reprinted by permission from *Faith At Work* Magazine, April 1972)

SOURCES

Foreword
1. Bernard Harnik, *Risk and Chance in Marriage* (Waco, Tex.: Word Books, 1972), p. 33.
2. David R. Mace, *Getting Ready for Marriage* (Nashville: Abingdon Press, 1972), p. 25.

Chapter 1: The Abbotts
1. Charlie W. Shedd, *Letters to Karen* (Nashville: Abingdon Press, 1965), p. 13.
2. Paul Tournier, *To Understand Each Other* (Atlanta: John Knox Press, 1967), p. 13.
3. Bernard R. Wiese and Urban G. Steinmetz, *Everything You Need to Know to Stay Married and Like It* (Grand Rapids: Zondervan Publishing House, 1972), p. 20.
4. Richard H. Klemer, *Marriage and Family Relationships* (New York: Harper and Row, 1970), p. 68.
5. David W. Augsburger, *Seventy Times Seven* (Chicago: Moody Press, 1970), pp. 97–98.

Chapter 2: The Parsonses
1. Klemer, *Marriage and Family Relationships,* p. 68.
2. Adapted from a list by Henry A. Bowman, *Marriage for Moderns* (New York: McGraw-Hill, 1960, 1965), pp. 388–90.
3. Lionel Whiston, *Are You Fun to Live With?* (Waco, Tex.: Word Books, 1968), pp. 118–19.
4. Dwight Hervey Small, *After You've Said I Do* (Old Tappan, N.J.: Fleming H. Revell Company, 1968), p. 122.

5. Klemer, *Marriage and Family Relationships*, p. 262.
6. Evelyn Duvall and Reuben Hill, *Being Married* (New York: Association Press, 1960), p. 251.

Chapter 3: The Reddicks
1. Howard J. Clinebell and Charlotte H. Clinebell, *The Intimate Marriage* (New York: Harper and Row, 1970), p. 69.
2. For more details, see *Why Marriage*, by Edward E. Ford (Niles, Ill.: Argus Communications, 1974), pp. 82 ff.
3. David W. Augsburger, *Caring Enough to Confront* (Glendale, Calif.: Regal Books, 1974), p. 74.
4. Available from John Knox Press, Atlanta, Ga.

Chapter 4: The Gilbertsons
1. As quoted in *Faith at Work* Magazine, April 1974, p. 8.
2. Charlie W. Shedd, *Letters to Philip* (Garden City, N.Y.: Doubleday, 1968), pp. 81–82.

Chapter 5: The Dominys
1. Klemer, *Marriage and Family Relationships*, pp. 185–87.
2. Charlie W. Shedd, *Letters to Karen* (Nashville: Abingdon Press, 1965), p. 105.
3. Klemer, *Marriage and Family Relationships*, p. 237.
4. Wiese and Steinmetz, *Everything You Need to Know to Stay Married and Like It*, p. 20.
5. Joseph and Lois Bird, *The Freedom of Sexual Love* (Garden City, N.Y.: Doubleday, 1970), p. 189.
6. Suggested by L. Richard Lessor, *From Married to Merried* (Niles, Ill.: Argus Communications, 1972), p. 27.
7. Shedd, *Letters to Karen*, pp. 37–39.

Chapter 6: The Chiltons
1. Clinebells, *The Intimate Marriage*, p. 25.
2. Robert Bower, *Solving Problems in Marriage* (Grand Rapids, Mich.: Wm. B. Eerdmans Publishing Company, 1972), p. 17.
3. Shedd, *Letters to Karen*, p. 111.
4. Clinebells, *The Intimate Marriage*, pp. 37–38.

Chapter 7: The Steffans
1. David W. Augsburger, *Cherishable: Love and Marriage* (Scottdale, Pa.: Herald Press, 1971), p. 53.
2. Paul Tournier as quoted in *The Living Marriage* by H. Norman Wright (Old Tappan, N.J.: Fleming H. Revell Company, 1975), p. 65.
3. Harnik, *Risk and Chance in Marriage*, pp. 172–73. cf. Rom. 12:10.
4. Theodor Bovet, *A Handbook to Marriage* (Garden City, N.Y.: Doubleday, 1969), p. 125.
5. Klemer, *Marriage and Family Relationships*, p. 190.

Chapter 8: The Pestanos
1. See *Why Marriage,* by Edward E. Ford (Niles, Ill.: Argus Communications, 1974).
2. Augsburger, *Caring Enough to Confront,* p. iii.
3. Tournier, *To Understand Each Other,* p. 29.
4. Harnik, *Risk and Chance in Marriage,* p. 79.

Chapter 9: The Claxtons
1. Paul Tournier, *Secrets* (Richmond, Va.: John Knox Press, 1965), p. 50.
2. Clinebells, *The Intimate Marriage,* p. 219.
3. C. S. Lewis, *The Four Loves* (London: Geoffrey Bles, 1960), pp. 121–22.

Chapter 10
1. John Powell, S.J., *The Secret of Staying in Love* (Niles, Ill.: Argus Communications, 1974), p. 13.
2. Quoted in the journal *Marriage,* Vol. 49, No. 1 (January, 1967), p. 37.